at home

IN SWEDEN 1900–2000

UUVE SNIDARE

TRANSLATED BY MARTIN HEAP

prisma

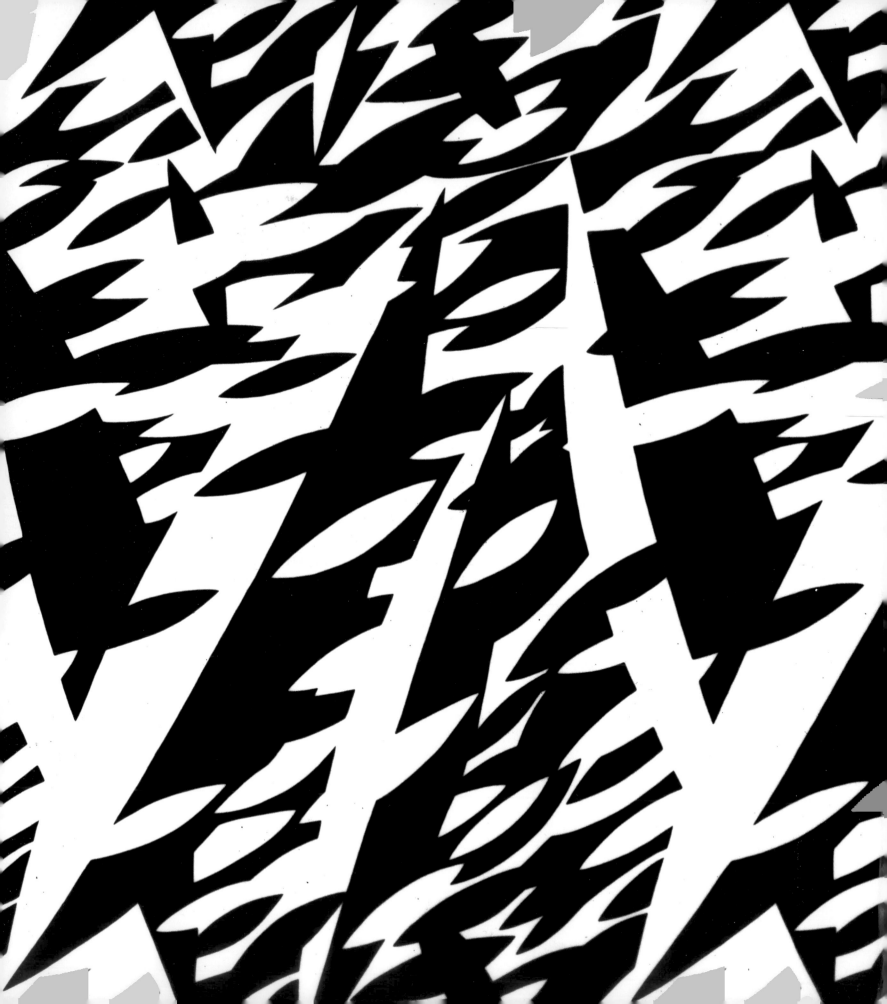

P

Bokförlaget Prisma
Visiting address: Tryckerigatan 4
Box 2052, 103 12 Stockholm, Sweden
prisma@prismabok.se
www.prismabok.se
Bokförlaget Prisma is a division of
P.A.Norstedt & Söner AB, founded in 1823

©Uuve Snidare and Bokförlaget Prisma 2000, 2002
Photography: Nisse Peterson, other photos see page 223
Designer: Oscar Snidare
English translation: Martin Heap
Original title: Hemma – i Sverige 1900–2000

Printed in Italy 2002
ISBN: 91-518-4068-5

Contents

Preface

The American philosopher Ralph Emerson once said: "All beauty reposes on the foundations of necessity".

Well, almost all.

Beauty in itself, without any sediment of necessity, does exist. The lapping of waves on a beach of shells, the shadow of a flower, a dance...

Even necessity in itself exists. Brutal survival, unreflecting functionalism. Who can claim that a basement garage is beautiful? But the human eye is demanding, and wants more. It wants to beautify the necessity of living. Here, Emerson is right.

It was when I began to study the functions of the home from the 20th century to the 21st, that I began to realise just how much our ideals of living have changed. From necessary, to gaudy, to functional, harmonious, beautiful. Dark, light. Open, enclosed. From having been one of the poorest countries in Europe with very overcrowded living conditions, we raised our standards in the home, through phenomenal willpower, to become an example to the world.

Cramped one-roomed flats, the "One Million Homes" programme, modular housing, self-owned homes, spacious loft-apartments, compact living, have succeeded each other. Trends have come and gone, from Art Nouveau, to Functionalism, to the chipboard of the 1970s. But most people, regardless of where they have lived, have always tried to beautify their homes. Starting from their own ideals, the fashion of the times, or the influence of media. A blue chequered cloth, or an elegantly designed expensive artefact – both with the same value.

You have only to compare the homes in *The Stucco Craftsman's House* and *Travelling Light into the 21st Century* for the difference to become clear.

During my journey from the late 19th century to the beginning of the 21st, I have documented thirty or so homes, from the extravagantly furnished house to simple cottages. Homes of the famous as well as of large, anonymous families. But all of them inventive and interesting in their own ways. It is a matter of personal choice.

I have given each decade a history: its designers, objects, architects, housing policies and the general spirit of the time. With, of course, a survey of international prototypes and inspirations.

Join me on my furnishing tour and see how and why we have lived – and live – as we do.

Uuve Snidare

Turn of the Century 1900

In the dark age of miscellany

Once upon a time there was a small, dark room. The walls were covered with sombre embossed wallpaper. Two layers of curtains hung in the windows, a thinner curtain nearer the glass and a dark burgundy, almost brown, velvet drape on the inside towards the room. Gloomy mustard-yellow, or rather oxidised-gold, tassels and edgings glowed dully in the light from outside. The furniture was in dark oak, the surface of the writing desk and chair were covered with worn and shiny brownish-black leather and several embroidered textiles lay over the rocking chair – a cover, a cushion and an antimacassar, all in gloomy autumnal colours, colours bordering on decay. Black-framed etchings, a standard lamp with a spirally-turned stand and blood-red fringed shade, and a palm on a pedestal completed the room. The description would fit August Strindberg's study just as well as any other literature-orientated bourgeois at the end of the 19th century. Strindberg himself was not entirely enamoured with these sepulchral residences and once proclaimed didactically in a poem: "tear it down to let in light and air!"

If he was calling for more light and air purely physically or also mentally is not clear, but certainly there was an accumulated desire for a lighter style, in all aspects of decoration and furnishing, after the late-century miscellany of styles and National Romantic inspiration.

New winds were soon to blow, but the majority of the town population still wished to shut out light, nature and unwholesome fresh air – with tuberculosis fresh in memory.

Living quarters were turned into caves where layer was laid upon layer, of both furniture and patterned textiles. Every surface was covered so that rooms became like a kaleidoscope. In this way, they are evocative of Arabic houses with their almost manic desire

to decorate every surface, the difference being that Arabic houses have white as their base.

Naturally it was not healthy to live in this way. Neither did author Ellen Key think so as she sat in her airy house, Strand, by Lake Vättern, nor the artists Karin and Carl Larsson when they moved with their seven children in 1901 to live permanently in their summer house at Sundborn in Dalarna.

At the end of the 19th century Carl Larsson had already begun painting watercolours of his home in revolutionary light and airy colours with, for those times, a shocking but captivatingly mundane slovenliness of motive. The book *Ett hem* (*A Home*) became a bestseller in Germany and gradually also well loved in Sweden, due not least to Ellen Key's promotion.

Ellen Key, the first woman to publicly demand female suffrage, was a keen propagandist both for the rights of children and women, but also an advocate of a light and simple home – an aesthetic she practised at Strand. White-painted furniture, potted plants indoors, rag-mats and an aesthetic but practically equipped kitchen have made her home a piece of well-preserved and much-visited history. Today it is both a museum and a guesthouse for female researchers.

Ellen Key published her propagandising book *Skönhet för alla* (*Beauty for Everyone*) at the turn of the 20th century, but as early as 1897 she had thundered in the magazine Idun: "A living room should not be a showpiece dominated by the most agonising order and the most pronounced luxury. When there is nothing ugly to buy, and the beautiful is as cheap as the ugly, first then can beauty for everyone become full reality."

She took her theses, like the Larssons, from the English designer and socialist William Morris, who claimed that beauty ennobles mankind. William Morris and John Ruskin pursued their aesthetics as part of their social programme, with an end to safeguarding the importance of craftsmanship in the age of new industrialism, which they claimed produced only quantity and not quality.

Above: Alf Wallander designed this white furniture for his house in Stocksund as early as 1899. The blue, red and white tablecloth decorated with Jugend style herons is from the same year.

Middle, left: Cast-iron furniture became popular at the turn of the 20th century. This is a French garden chair.

Middle, right: The famous "Viennese chair" was created in the 1860s by Michel Thonet and has since been produced in millions.

Left: Ellen Key's home, Strand, by Lake Vättern, is a vivid example of the new, light and simple lifestyle that both she and the Larssons advocated. This white rocking chair stands in the living room.

Old styles are mixed

The turn of the century was a turning point. During the later 19th century the so-called New Styles, a concoction of old stylistic ideals, succeeded each other – New Gothic, New Baroque, Dutch Renaissance. Finally the new, independent Jugend style, or Art Nouveau, as it was called in France, with its billowy ornamented forms in cement and cast-iron, furniture and graphic design. The contemporary Swedish and National Romantic ideal revealed itself in buildings and furniture as a mixture of Jugend and chauvinistically Swedish idioms, with much granite, cast-cement portals, pilasters formed like pine trunks, but also with softly formed ornaments of pine-cones, wild flowers and oak leaves.

Carl Westman, also an important furniture designer, was one of the great architects of the time; a cheerful person who, with his painter wife Elin, reminded one of the Larssons at Sunborn. The Westmans also left their city life for a more romantic way of life in the country at nearby Saltsjöbaden. Carl Westman designed many houses in the area, homes that he also created the furniture for. The most successful of these are the simple Windsor-style chairs and sofas that were glazed in green or dark-red – shocking at the time. But it was also Westman who designed the heavy stone fortresses of Stockholm's Law Courts and the Röhsska Craft Museum in Gothenburg.

Many other large stone buildings were built during this time, preferably using Swedish granite. The new bourgeoisie needed housing for their administration, banks, schools and factories. And also for accommodation.

Seven in one room

The turn of the century was a time of great change. Industrialism speeded up and with it came massive migration to the towns, which were not dimensioned for such an influx. Living conditions became very overcrowded. Six to seven people in one old-fashioned room was not unusual. Amongst them was often a lodger, to help with the rent.

It was, in fact, worse here than in the country, since there was no wood for fuel nearby, the privy across the yard was shared with many others and the possibility of giving the children fresh vegetables and water was limited. This was the age of bedbugs and tuberculosis. The working class home was primarily a place to sleep – several to each bed and the small children in drawers. Food was cooked on wood burning stoves and the washing was dried above it. You can imagine how it looked. At the end of the 19th century a man could say: "Home is a hell, while the pub and the brothel are heavens of cleanliness and space"!

A survey made in 1897 of the living accommodation in Stockholm's inner city showed, alarmingly, that half the population lived in flats of one room and a kitchen, or less, and of these 47 percent had a lodger! Only a fifth of the workers had two rooms and

a kitchen, but often one of the rooms was rented out. It was not until the 1920s that small flats started to get their own toilet and bathroom.

Considering the difficult living situation one can understand that the typical working-class home was sparsely furnished, more or less like rural labourers' cottages – a table, one or two chairs, a chest of drawers and a pull-out sofa. The bedclothes, for those without a bed and sleeping on the floor, were kept in a trunk.

If you climb up the class-ladder you get a new picture of the home and its furnishing. Here, there is money to invest in furniture whose first purpose is to emulate the furniture of the rich. The apartments become stage-sets with drawing rooms, smoking rooms, gloomy dining rooms and sometimes a library. The kitchen and the nursery – where the real life is lived – were banished to small box-rooms facing the dingy back yards. In these rooms furnishing is still very meagre, but since no guests come here, they need not be shown. That children fared badly in this dark, narrow environment was of lesser importance.

Below: The dining room at Karin and Carl Larsson's home Sundborn is in green and subdued red – a popular colour combination that William Morris also fostered. The home was revolutionarily modern for its time.

Previous spread: The turn of the century wallpaper glows dully and is mirrored in the shiny surface of the grand piano. The statuette proclaims an interest in the Oriental.

The Stucco Craftsman's House

The punsch veranda, mahogany, palms on pedestals, jet necklaces and hats with ostrich feathers, parasols, dark drapes. One does not need to say more to conjure up a picture of the turn of the 20th century interior.

One of the more elegant and completely preserved interiors is the so-called Stucco Craftsman's House on David Bagares Street in Stockholm. The stucco craftsman was Axel Notini, who came from an Italian craft family. Through his marriage to his master's daughter Augusta, he obtained both the plot of land and money as a wedding present. Notini himself partly designed the house in the 1880s and decorated both the façade and the interior with fantastic stucco work. You have to go and knock the surface, in fact, to discover that it is plaster and not wood, metal or stone.

Axel Notini used the house as his "portfolio". He often invited important people to his home, therefore, and soon became Stockholm's most esteemed stucco worker. Amongst other things he has done the ornamentation of Grand Hôtel's large dining room, the entrance to the Arvfursten's Palace and the stucco work at Rosendal Palace.

The Stucco Craftsman's House is built in three storeys with an open staircase in the middle, enclosed with glass at the top. The show apartment is on the middle floor, with all the furnishings of the time. Dark, hand-printed wallpaper of gold leather. Several layers of curtains and drapes. All furniture is of oak and mahogany or other dark stained wood with hard upholstered sofas and armchairs. Crochet antimacassars lie over the backs of the sofas, some white, others in rather loud colour combinations.

Left and above: The study was also Mr. Notini's office. The walls are dark burgundy with paintings by contemporary artists, many of them frequent visitors to the house. The colour scale is dark-green and burgundy, and one wonders how the obligatory palm could survive in such gloom. You have to zigzag between one-legged tables and etageres for trinkets. His writing table is of walnut, covered with embossed black leather. Writing equipment, a watch, glasses and a telephone are close at hand.

Previous spread, right: The dining table gleams in preparation for a sumptuous party. The chandelier and the candelabra are lit, the serviettes folded and each place has at least four glasses of cut crystal. The heavy dark-green tile stove spreads its warmth from the corner. The doors and doorways are moulded by the stucco master's own hand, even if they look just like wood. Everything is painted in different dark shades highlighted with gold leaf. The taste for Jugend can be seen in the tall oak chairs and in the candlesticks on the sideboard.

Previous spread, left: The abundance of objects is typical for the turn of the 20th century home. The lady's dressing table in the bedroom is no exception. It is crowded with ornaments, jewellery and textiles.

The interiors are richly decorated and every surface is covered with objects. Cut-glass chandeliers, paraffin lamps and candelabra jostle with each other. This was partly a wealthy home, partly a fashionable gloom, which was necessary to light up even on cloudy days in summer.

Notini was modern for his time and was one of the first to install a telephone – a fantastically ornate object standing on the writing table. He even installed gas as soon as it came at the end of the 19th century. The Bolinder stove in the kitchen looks like a conventional cast-iron stove but it has large pipes and white taps for the gas.

According to the city plan of 1967, the Stucco Craftsman's House was due to be demolished. This was during our latest era of "air and light" when the whole of the old city was to be razed to the ground, to emerge again as a modern concrete town. This did not happen and the St Erik Society bought the stucco craftsman's apartment and donated it to the town of Stockholm which administers it today. The Stockholm Town Museum decided to turn it into a museum apartment in 1997. The Town Museum has devoted much time to a meticulous refurbishment of the stucco craftsman's apartment. It is now open for guided tours.

Left: Despite the great amount of entertaining the Notini family did, they had to make do with the ultramodern gas stove in the corner of the kitchen but no working surfaces at all. The chamfered tiles above the stove are the same as those used on the walls of the Metro in Paris.

Right: Arrack punsch put out to cool on the serving bench in the kitchen corridor together with a neat row of glasses. You can see out through the lace curtain into the stairwell. This let you see who was coming, and also provided indirect light from the large roof-window in the stairwell. All the woodwork is done by skilled craftsmen and painted in a pleasant grey-umber tone.

Captain Jönsson's
Home in Viken

One can feel sorry for Captain Paul and his wife Hilda Jönsson in Viken. The couple moved to a long, low building on Skeppargatan near the centre of Viken at the end of the 19th century. Paul Jönsson, who had always dreamt of life at sea, sailed for many years around Europe and further, on the modern steamship *Kattegatt*. He and Hilda had four children during their life, but only one grandchild. Both sons were killed in unnecessary and dramatic ways – one was drowned and one accidentally shot himself. One daughter, Lily, emigrated to America and came back at the end of her life, childless. The other married and had a daughter who also emigrated to America. Even her husband died, during a trip to Norway.

So all the presents that Paul Jönsson brought home from his many and long trips remained in his and Hilda's house.

The house on Skeppargatan is preserved exactly as it looked in 1904, when the captain had finished his seafaring. His six small rooms are crowded with furniture, as was usual at the turn of the 20th century. The captain had his own bedroom and study at one end of the house. Here in these dark, masculine rooms are most of his seafaring mementoes – shells, meerschaum pipes, small statues, porcelain, tins and books in foreign languages. The walls in the large drawing room, which is, in fact, not particularly large, are covered in golden brown imitation velour wallpaper. Even the furniture and types of wood are of different shades of brown. There are bowls, jars, porcelain dogs and paraffin lamps. It is chock-full.

They lived there during the whole period without any modern facilities. With no water or drains, with coal-fired stoves and light from paraffin lamps. Hilda changed the latter in the early 1920s, but this was the only modernity that ever came into the house. Hilda herself was very skilful with needle and thread, and the drawers are

Left: Hilda's bed is a wonder of textile art. Lace-inset pillowcases, monograms and flowery embroidery on the sheets, and a skilfully crocheted bedspread of fine cotton thread. Even the thin black-and-white plaid is home-woven.

Below: The coal-fired stoves were never replaced by a more modern heating system. But the shining cast-iron stove in the corner is certainly handsome. A painted ostrich egg is hanging from it – a memento from the Captain's travels.

Previous spread: It was here in the drawing room in the middle of the house that they received guests, drank coffee and conversed. Presumably they wanted the Captain's journeys to impress somewhat, since all the mementoes from different countries are piled on top of each other, along with local earthenware from Höganäs and textiles made by Hilda.

full of the most exquisite embroidery on cloths, sheets and pillow-cases. Even her own bedding in the small bedroom is an eldorado for those interested in textiles. Not to mention the clothes in the wardrobe! On the other hand, what was she to do, with her husband at sea and her children gone?

In the small dining room next to the kitchen is a portrait of the emigrated grandchild Dagny. It is exotically framed with shells and hangs against wallpaper that is a Swedish classic and is still in production. All the textiles in the room are woven by Hilda, who had her own loom in a house in the back yard.

The Captain's house is a typical, if somewhat simple, bourgeois home from that period. You can see it in the mixture of the elegant and the ordinary, by the way the etchings and marine paintings are hung high and spaciously on the walls. Even the small hallway into the yard, where they took off their clogs and washed their hands – and in the evenings their whole bodies – is testimony to their relatively simple circumstances, despite the somewhat ostentatious dining room.

Above: The hall at the back is also the "bathroom". They took off their clogs here and washed their hands before meals. But they also did all their personal hygiene in this narrow, cold space next to the garden!

Right: The small dining room, or the Room, as it was called, and where they really spent their time, is abundant with textiles. Not in the town fashion but in a more countrified way, since Hilda herself wove. A photo of their grandchild, Dagny, hangs on the wall in a kitschy shell frame.

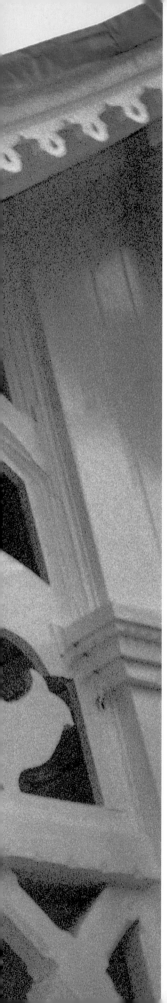

1900–1910

An aesthetic of light takes root

All talk about aesthetics and technology during the first decade of the century gradually transforms into a manifesto and concrete action. William Morris and John Ruskin have been propagating abroad for good craftsmanship as an antithesis to industrialism's "vulgar products". Morris designs both wallpaper and textile patterns with light, ornamental botanical motives – patterns that are still produced and loved by many. The English Arts and Craft Movement publish The Studio magazine, with modern ideas about colour, form and living. Karin and Carl Larsson in Sweden are particularly influenced by them.

The Jugend, or Art Nouveau, designer Henry van de Velde in Belgium follows Ruskin's and Morris's ideas. Another social-radical movement grows in Austria, the so-called Secession, lead by Otto Wagner, Josef Hoffman, Gustav Klimt and Koloman Moser. Josef Hoffman and Otto Wagner at the Wiener Werkstätte, in 1903, also create designs with a view to supporting good craftsmanship. But it is not a question of copying old styles or even Jugend. They are more possibly influenced by Classicism, and with this European Modernism is born.

At the same time, in "that little hole Glasgow in Scotland", furniture and furnishings are being created by Charles Rennie Mackintosh of such originality that he comes to embody the real Modernism. He is doing this during the first decade of the 20th century, relatively uninfluenced by Central European currents. His most famous work is the Glasgow School of Art, completed in 1909, which is totally his own work, from the façade to the smallest keyhole. Even the black chairs with their high, straight backs in latticed patterns are among his famous masterpieces.

Rather Carl Larsson than Modernism

Modernism came to Sweden more stealthily. We can see the new, simple furniture in a pared-down style by Carl Westman, Alf Wallander, Carl Bergsten amongst others. Carl Westman develops the Swedish National Romantic Style from heavy, German-inspired chairs and sofas in oak or green and red glazes, into light, white furniture with the Swedish Windsor-style chair as a model.

The rounded forms in Alf Wallander's furniture and porcelain are similar to the swelling European and graceful Jugend style, particularly of the type represented by Henry van de Velde. Carl Bergsten, with his strict straight and oval shapes, comes closest to the modern furniture ideas of Mackintosh.

All the furniture and furnishings that were created in the beginning of the 20th century, and which we admire today, have usually been used by the so-called "discerning". Those who were already converted to the Modern and were careful to project themselves as liberal and forward-looking. The ordinary middle and working class man continues to use traditional furniture, mixing styles and trying to give an impression of living better than he really does.

Luckily Carl Larsson's watercolours were printed and universally spread. There was no better propagandist for the simple life. Gradually more and more people realised that it was neither ugly nor sinful to show that one lived naturally, with unmade beds, semiclothed children and living rooms that showed signs of both life and strife.

General education increased. Now the masses were to be enlightened. In the spirit of Ellen Key, with much stalwart and pointed advice. There was to be an end to the stupidity of keeping one room empty, as a front room, while the family squeezed into the kitchen for all their different activities, from cooking and washing to keeping company and sleeping. No, out with the heavy, polished parlour furniture and in with the simple, functional, easy-to-look-after furniture was the slogan.

One step forward, one step back

The first decade of the new century was in general a forward-looking period, a time when light and clear colours were discovered. But, like so much else, it did not last very long, or rather, went into decline. The Baltic Exhibition in Malmö in 1914, already pointed to a return to heavy, dark furniture in a style that imitated earlier epochs. The furniture had, however, a very high standard of craftsmanship. Much of it came from the new furniture producers, Gemla, Chambert and Giöbel. The only one to produce light furni-

Above: Charles Rennie Mackintosh created his simple, cubic and completely revolutionary chair of black, lacquered wood as early as 1903. He was a modernist, from backwater Glasgow, who went his own way and created a style that is vital even today.

Left: Dark wood dominated most homes. This wooden staircase with a built-in bookcase, designed by Ferdinand Boberg, is in the Grünewald Villa.

Previous spread: At the beginning of the century, both heavy granite houses and elegant summer houses, with a great deal of decoratively carved features, were built.

ture in its own style was the Swedish Handcraft Association. Their work was founded on the folklore tradition with its strong connection to genuine craftsmanship and local materials. Lilly Zickerman, the founder of Swedish Handcraft in 1899, had already made her adventurous, nation-wide trips to the North and South of Sweden, primarily to document the Swedish textile treasury. Twenty-four thousand textiles and sketches were catalogued as a result. This became the base of the rich knowledge of our roots that we have in Sweden, in contrast to most other countries.

Swedish Handcraft supplied its own shops with everything from curtains, furnishing fabrics, carpets and furniture, to utensils of pottery, wood and metal. This light and functional furniture had many buyers, both from companies and architects, and from ordinary people. Thanks to them, Carl Larsson's and Ellen Key's ideas for the home could be spread wider. Erik Folcker, who imported English fabrics and wallpapers from William Morris, amongst others, was another important figure. There was a large selection of these light and airy patterns at his shop, Sub Rosa, in Stockholm.

Right: Alf Wallander designed a room in late Jugend style for the Stockholm Exhibition of 1909. It featured high sofa cupboards with soft lines and a round table. Everything was in birch, and colours were autumnal.

Below: Well-known classic chairs from the turn of the century, several designed for mass production. Carl Westman, Ragnar Östberg, Carl Berglund, designed many of them.

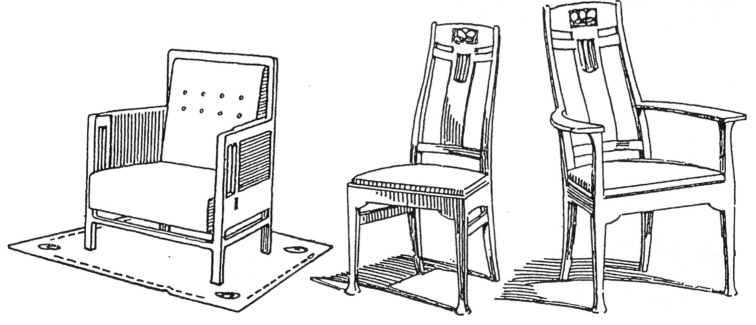

The dream of the archipelago villa

The dream of the summer home was born at the turn of the 20th century. Wealthy bourgeois families in growing towns procured country houses. Ideally, a white painted house in the archipelago with verandas, bay windows and towers – covered with skilful fretwork. In Stockholm's archipelago these were known as "wholesaler villas".

The rich children from the city could come here to play and breathe fresh air. The women, children and servants moved out here as soon as school finished and stayed until the beginning of the autumn term, while the men commuted. It would take another 30–40 years before the dream of the summer home could come true for ordinary people (see page 70).

Furnishings in the summer houses were of course simpler and lighter and clearly demonstrated the interest in nature of the Swedish people. This was expressed in the form of carved details, bulbous chair and table legs, woven textiles with stylised plant ornamentation – many from Handarbetets Vänner (The Friends of Handcraft) – and porcelain with beautiful floral decorations by Alf Wallander and Gunnar Wennerberg.

These richly decorated summer villas were often built in intimate collaboration between buyer and building contractor or architect. No two houses were to be the same, although with hindsight we feel that they have the same National Romantic style, whether they are on the East or the West Coast. Or beside a lake in Middle Sweden.

Emil Haeger, the owner of Lilla Edet's paper mill, created one such typical summer villa for himself and his family on the West coast at Lyckorna. It is called Villa Sjötorp. The parts were made at a carpentry factory in Lilla Edet and transported by barge to this sloping site at Havstens fjord, where they were quickly assembled, in 1901.

Villa Sjötorp is today, after several changes, back in the ownership of the same family and in use as a boarding house and restaurant.

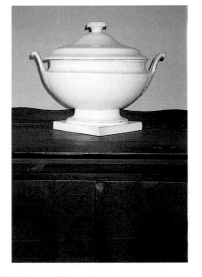

Left: Many of the bedrooms in the wealthy bourgeois summer homes looked like this; walls in off-white, a black iron bed and a palm on a pedestal. Beds were much narrower than today's, 60–80 centimetres.

Above: Villa Sjötorp at Lyckorna in the West Coast archipelago has quite broad barge boards in the triple ridged veranda roof.

Closest left: Mahogany, real or painted, was the popular material for furniture – unless it was given a modern white colour. But this was only in the summer houses. A cream ware terrine stands on the bureau.

Grünewald's White Drawing Room

Large wooden villas were built in what used to be the countryside at Saltsjöbaden outside Stockholm, with a view over Baggens fjord. One of these, Villa Lugnet, built by Ferdinand Boberg for the industrialist Knut Tillberg in 1883, was seen as rather modest, until publisher Hugo Geber took over in 1911. He let architect Carl Westman add a wing with, amongst other things, a new kitchen. When the artist Isaac Grünewald eventually acquired the house, the large studio was added and suddenly the villa, now known as the Grünewald Villa, had grown to 700 square metres. After many years of decay and even the threat of demolition, the house was bought in the 1980s by Johan Öhlin and is used today for exhibitions, conferences, private parties and so on.

The Grünewald Villa is a typical example of late 19th century buildings, with dark-brown wooden panelling, turrets and towers, balconies and bay windows. It stands like an eagle's nest looking down over the water and the nearby Grand Hôtel.

Even the large staircase inside is dark and heavy, like several of the halls and tower rooms, but in one of the drawing rooms, the White Room, the walls are white. There is a large glazed veranda at one end of this pleasantly light room. The veranda has a stone floor made with white and terracotta clinker tiles. The ceiling is four metres high and the large barred windows go right up to the ceiling on three sides. It is a unique room and excellent for exotic trees such as olives, bay trees, hibiscuses and lilies.

Exquisite furniture from 1910, of unknown origin but signed with an "L" on the bottom, stands on the slightly raised floor. The light sofa and both armchairs have ribbed backs and sides. The backs have a decorative circle, which is also filled with thin ribbing. The furniture is painted in a cream hue with contemporary oil-based paint. Several pedestals and a practical, small folding table form part of the furnishing, as well as several busts, including one of Lord Byron.

Right: One end of the White Room at the Grünewald Villa is formed as becomes a large veranda room, with light coming from three sides and a step up to the red and white clinker floor. You get the feeling of sitting outdoors as you take your afternoon coffee or tea on the graceful, cream three-piece suite from 1910. The designer is, unfortunately, unknown.

The 1910ˢ

Modernism and machine manufacture

After the Baltic Exhibition of 1914, with its many gloomy interiors in imitated styles, it was obvious that something had to be done to raise the "taste of the People". What craftsmanship could offer was made by hand and relatively expensive for the ordinary man. They had to start looking at mass production and factory manufacture.

Modernism had already been accepted abroad and co-operation had begun between the architect/designer and the manufacturer. This had resulted in completely new idioms and materials, at prices that were far lower than handmade products.

The De Stijl group was formed in Holland, consisting of architects, designers, painters and philosophers. The aim was to find a new style, not based on the forms of nature but an aesthetic based on machine design. They used bright colours and straight lines. The most famous example is Gerrit Rietveld's red and blue chair from 1918. It looks like a spillikins toy and is today a cult classic. Rietveld also built a house, Villa Schröder in Utrecht, which is a museum and a Mecca for those interested in the new architecture influenced by cubism and constructivism. The members of the De Stijl group experimented with geometrically disbanded forms and bright colours in the same way as the Russian constructivists El Lissitsky, Rodchenko and Kandinsky. In Russia, this was a time of openness and of breaching boundaries, whether in the design of textile patterns, posters and chinaware, or in Art.

By 1903, Henry Ford had founded his car factory in America. The model-T Ford was one of the first products made by machine,

Above: Uno Åhrén created this large kitchen for the controversial Home Exhibition at Liljevalchs in 1917. It featured white furniture, including a combined sofa/bed, and large worktops for washing-up, baking and food preparation. The kitchen was meant to be where the working family spent time together.

Left: The Swedish Craft Association was behind the Home Exhibition at Liljevalchs. The simplicity of the poster proclaims: We are exhibiting good homes for the less well-off.

Previous spread: Wilhelm Kåge was the great star at Gustavsberg. He designed his so-called working-class chinaware, Liljeblå, for the Home Exhibition. Here are some cups from that period, Liljeblå on the left.

with the parts being put together by hand on a conveyor belt. This made production much cheaper. Ford's ideas spread far and wide and for the first time one could talk of the mass-production of goods. Suddenly there were designers who realised that you could make good products despite the machines. For them function came first. The American architect Louis Sullivan coined the expression Form follows Function.

Swedish workers are wary

These were hard times for the Swedish worker. There were both general strikes and famine in the poor North, while the "profiteering barons" and other wealthy men lined their own pockets.

But things were slowly progressing with more and more people getting better housing and greater possibilities of influencing their own surroundings. Thus the demand for good everyday utensils grew steadily. These utensils had to work. They had to fit into small spaces. They preferably had to have several functions and last for a long time. Moreover they had to be beautiful! The debate that grew up had only two arguments: beautiful or ugly.

It was time for a new manifestation. An exhibition that would teach the people once and for all what is beautiful and what is ugly! This happens at the Hemutställningen (Home Exhibition) in 1917, at the newly built Liljevalchs Hall of Art designed by Carl Bergsten; the first real neo-classical building in Stockholm. The exhibition concentrates on dwellings with one or two rooms, designed primarily for workers. Twenty-three complete interiors were built in full scale. The architects Gunnar Asplund and Uno Åhrén received much attention for their large, light kitchens with generous space for eating and entertaining, and also with room for a rib-backed settee that could also be used as a bed. But despite the light furniture, the better working surfaces and the light curtains, they were criticised by women who questioned their practicability. Why not let in female interior designers, I wonder, if there were any?

The handcraft movement, led by its founder Lilly Zickerman, was dominated by women, after all. Textile artist Elsa Gullberg had started an agency to connect artists to producers of textiles and furniture, but they were kept to one side. Maybe they did not even want to get involved with the functions and designs of a kitchen.

But, yes, there was one woman, Sara Reuterskiöld, who designed an ideal kitchen for the exhibition Bygge och Bo (Building and Living) in 1924. This was also presented in the book for housewives: *Om kök och köksinredningar (About Kitchens and Kitchen Equipment)*, 1927. She complains that the woman/housewife comes into the planning at far too late a stage, when the architect had already decided the basic plan with its placing of windows, piping and plumbing. This leaves the housewife with only the surface to concern herself with, she says in vexation.

Sara Reuterskiöld's kitchen has the cooker near the window, for the light. There are two sinks; one for rough jobs and one for washing-up and food preparation. An ingenious baking-table can be pulled out like a quarter-circle in the corner of the worktop, and a padded cupboard door can be let down as an ironing board.

In most areas, however, men prevailed. They took the social and aesthetic responsibility upon themselves and, at the same time, credit for bringing modernity to the country. Wilhelm Kåge, at the Gustavsberg porcelain factory, designed so-called working-class chinaware. He wanted, in true social spirit, to give ordinary people an alternative to the over-decorated, cheaply patterned "fine cups" that flooded in from abroad. Kåge's dinner service Liljeblå did become popular, but not amongst those whom he had hoped. The aesthetically conscious bought them, but not the workers. You did not get enough for your money, they argued. For it was not especially cheap, being made in Sweden and of good materials. The indefatigable Kåge continued to create a whole series of dishes and bowls, Praktika, which could be stacked very practically into each other. Even these were bought by the "wrong target group", despite the fact that overcrowding was the biggest problem, which should have lead to a demand for functional and compact products. The ovenproof service Pyro, shown at the Stockholm Exhibition in 1930, was a great success, however.

The Home Exhibition in 1917 was nevertheless significant. Carl Malmsten had his break-through, exhibiting an interior with dark lacquered furniture and many textiles. Dark furniture was suddenly seen to be the most practical for the overcrowded!

Rounding off the decennium, two years after the Home Exhibition, Gregor Paulsson, the debater and art historian, published the pamphlet *Vackrare vardagsvara (Beauty in Everyday Utensils)*. This was the Swedish Handcraft Association's first polemical publication, in which Gregor Paulsson discusses beauty and ugliness. He claimed that bad taste is a national disease: "People's curiosity and respect for shop-sold mouth organs and neckties and shawls are similar to the savage's for glass pearls. When the savage becomes civilised, the sickness passes". But there were also less brutal assertions. Gregor Paulsson believes that the

machine can be used in a good way, with a more efficient use of materials, less time-consuming and thereby cheaper. And above all, he argued, the artist had to be brought into the process.

"The object will be both well-suited and beautiful only if a person educated for the purpose creates the form or the decoration", he writes. "And only then will we get away from the false imitations and historical styles that lie like an oppressive nightmare over architecture and decorative art."

So true!

Left: This garden chair is made of compressed metal with a wooden seat and was manufactured in the1920s by the French company Société Industrielle des Meubles Multiples – mass production which, in its form and rationality, heralds the plastic chairs of the 1960s and 1970s.

Below: The artist Einar Hylander associated the white furniture style with the summers of his childhood. In 1980 he re-created a completely white home with a feeling of space and light, in a backyard in Stockholm. Everything is built by hand and with simple resources. Today the home is a museum.

The 1920s

A golden age for Swedish architecture

Things now start happening, both indoors and outdoors. Jugend, or Art Nouveau, has waned a long time ago and people have become Modern in many ways. We get a social democratic government and universal suffrage in 1921. Skirts go up, long hair is cut off. The stage is set for the "free" woman who can stand on her own two feet and step out into the workplace. The jazz comes from America and the Functionalist currents from Germany.

In Sweden, where we are not quite so daring, a calm and beautiful neo-classicism evolves. Buildings with formal elements from both classical antiquity and the Renaissance begin to appear, amongst others the Stockholm Concert Hall with its classical row of columns facing the Haymarket, designed by Ivar Tengbom and completed in 1926. Another is Stockholm's Town Hall by Ragnar Östberg in 1923, famous not least for its exquisitely floating situation, almost on the water. But Gunnar Asplund has already created a milestone in 1918 – the famous Villa Snellman at Djursholm in neo-classical style.

The 1920s and 1930s could rightly be called the golden age of Swedish architecture. They see a new world on the horizon and erect buildings for this new era. The architect is allowed to take a comprehensive grasp, from the whole volume and the exterior decoration, down to the smallest detail indoors. A trust that has since been successively undermined. The architect Sven Wallander founded HSB (the National Association of Tenants' Savings and Building Societies) in 1923, and several housing projects were built under its auspices that are still seen as good prototypes: Helgalunden, Blecktornsparken and Röda Bergen in Stockholm, Kungsladugård in Gothenburg and Södra Kvarngärde in Uppsala. The flats are still small but they are built with good materials, larger windows with few bars and often an open fireplace. Bathrooms and refuse chutes are standard, something which is seen as a great luxury.

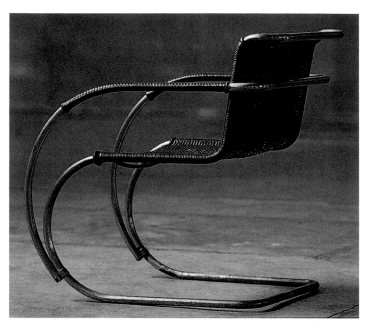

Above: Many designers used modernistic tubular steel during the 1920s. The most elegant was probably Ludwig Mies van der Rohe's springy chair, MR 20, with a basketwork seat, designed in 1927. Later, it was also made with a leather seat.

Below, left: Bauhaus and tubular steel are forever associated with each other, regardless of where they were designed and produced. The picture shows a chair by Eskil Sundahl and an anonymous standard lamp from Germany. Both from the 1930s.

Below, right: Thin, heat-resistant Jena glass also characterises the 1930s. This elegant tea service was designed in 1931 by Sutnar Ladislav in Czechoslovakia. The teapot has a metal ring with an elegant handle made of black wood.

Previous spread: The international functionalist style first reached Sweden at the end of the 1920s. These white houses in Södra Ängby, Stockholm, are an example.

Swedish grace

Furniture and furnishings display a classical restraint, something that leads to many international prizes, and the phrase Swedish Grace is coined. Amongst the designers is the young and assertive Carl Malmsten, who makes light furniture with roots in Swedish tradition. He gets large commissions for interior design from both the state and ordinary people. His furniture is almost as relevant today as it was then, at any rate in traditional homes. Malmsten's opposite was the modernist Gunnar Asplund, who becomes the representative of Swedish Functionalism, and makes experimental furniture using steel tubing, amongst other materials, something for which he is praised in Paris. His now world-famous City Library in Stockholm is opened at the end of the 1920s. A building that combines a monumental outer form – the cylinder on the cube – with a light and airy interior, heralding a whole new way of thinking.

The young artists Simon Gate and Edward Hald come to the Orrefors glass foundry in 1916 and 1917. They create new ways of working with glass, both polished cut-glass and grail glass, with vigorous courage and great freedom. Hald, who had been a pupil of Matisse, engraves humorous and startling modern decorations on his large bowls, urns and vases. He also works for Rörstrands, the ceramic factory. The artist Wilhelm Kåge, working for Gustavsberg, paints faience and inserts silver intarsia into green-glazed objects – Argenta. The public at the Paris handcraft exhibition in 1925 are ecstatic over all this new work, elegant but also playful. The three artists are awarded the Grand Prix and many gold medals, while the newspapers speak admiringly of Swedish Grace.

But how did people live at the time? This is still the period before the great rupture – before Functionalism. But the more airy flats invite a lighter style of furniture. Thanks to the debate about taste, the manufacturers that deliver furniture to the department store NK, David Blomberg and the Swedish Furniture Factories, worked with neo-classical forms. The Swedish Windsor-style chair, wicker furniture, and lighter, more flexible solutions are in fashion. Even wallpaper becomes lighter. Uno Åhrén, Gunnar Asplund and Carl Malmsten all design light, blue-white wallpaper. Curtains turn white. Karin and Carl Larsson's aesthetic seems to have finally broken through.

Bauhaus and Functionalism

Great things are happening abroad. Modernism with its passion for the functional develops into an even more dominating style thanks to the German design school Bauhaus, founded by Walter Gropius at Weimar in 1919, and moved to Dessau in 1925. It was shut down in 1933 by Hitler, who felt threatened by the geometric, abstract and "decadent" creativity there.

The great artists, architects and constructors of the time gather at Bauhaus and a new profession, that of the Designer, is born. They preach fidelity to materials and call for a universal language for the designed object. Art co-operates with technology. The theoretical discussion is important. A new, rationally-directed world is to be created, where mass production will serve the people. New materials in the form of steel, glass and concrete are seen as the foundation for the aesthetic of living. Louis Sullivan's slogan, "Form follows Function" fits perfectly, as does Mies van der Rohe's "Less is More".

The teachers at Bauhaus include artists and architects such as Wassily Kandinsky, Paul Klee, Johannes Itten, Ludwig Mies van der Rohe. The list of famous designers who attended the school and who later, at the end of the decade, disseminated the ideas and forms of Functionalism, is even longer.

Art Déco the Scandinavian way

A new movement was launched at the Paris Exposition Internationale des Arts Décoratifs et Industriels Modernes in 1925: Art Déco – a kind of streamlined and decorative Modernism. It was clearly influenced by the latest expressions of Art: Cubism and Constructivism. The Russians also had their own large area at the exhibition, as did Le Corbusier who showed a Cubist – naturally decried – modular building: the L'Esprit Nouveau pavilion.

The Finland-Swedish architect Pauli Blomsted was inspired by Bauhaus Functionalism, but added streamlined details, similar to the French features at the Paris exhibition, in his own design. Using black and dark terracotta, tubular steel and leather, he worked with the elements of tension between straight and curved forms.

His nephew's wife, the interior designer Kaisa Blomsted, lives in one of Helsinki's first functionalist apartment blocks. She has re-created Pauli Blomsted's spirit in her flat, using objects and furniture from the 1920s and 1930s. Many of them are his own designs, mixed with Italian design and other exclusive contemporary work.

Above: The furniture in this Helsinki apartment is mostly designed by Pauli Blomsted. The small two-tier table is newly reproduced by Merivaara's furniture factory. Even the other features – the mirror, radio, vases and other ornaments – are contemporary.

Left: The kitchen furniture is of modern Kaisa Blomsted design, but inspired by Art Déco. The masur birch doors have been given decorative black handles and are mounted in black wooden frames. The opal-white glass behind the working surface provides a pleasant light for working. The floor has black and white linoleum tiles – very modern at that time!

Below: The music room in Kaisa Blomsted's Art Déco apartment has an old black piano, with a modern uplight in the corner. The rustic black and walnut table from the 1930s can be extended. The 1930s armchairs are covered with fabric designed by Aino Aalto, Alvar Aalto's first wife.

The 1930s

Functionalism's breakthrough in Sweden

The 1920s were drawing to a close and functionalist currents from abroad were growing ever stronger. Many Swedish designers and architects had already begun working with austere forms and new materials such as tubular steel, glass and concrete. Glass was no longer seen purely as a material for letting in daylight, but also as a feature for use in large unbroken surfaces. As decorative parts of the exterior. Concrete replaced heavy brick in walls, which allowed for sleeker buildings with smooth, white surfaces. Steel was a willing component of both buildings and furniture.

The result was that the new buildings appeared to be both floating and well anchored at the same time. Like white Atlantic liners stranded on land. Houses were often cubic with windows giving life to the façade, with flat roofs and with horizontally railed balconies. Large glass-enclosed entrances and open stairways with carefully worked banisters of bentwood or tubular steel were also common features. All the stucco was gone, as was all ornamentation and embellishment in the form of bay windows, towers and extra angles.

The most famous Swedish architects were Sven Markelius, who designed a house for communal living on NorrMälarstrand in Stockholm on the initiative of Alva Myrdal, and Gunnar Asplund who designed the Stockholm City Library and the Forest Cemetery (in co-operation with Sigurd Lewerentz). Eskil Sundahl and Olof Thunström, working at the architects' office of KF (the Swedish Cooperative Union and Wholesale Society), created many residential houses and public buildings, not least a large number of co-op stores. Artur von Schmalensee also designed the Luma factory in Stockholm for KF.

KF's architects' office was the largest in Scandinavia during the 1930s and the most influential, with its group of visionary, young architects. This office created plans not only for inexpensive houses

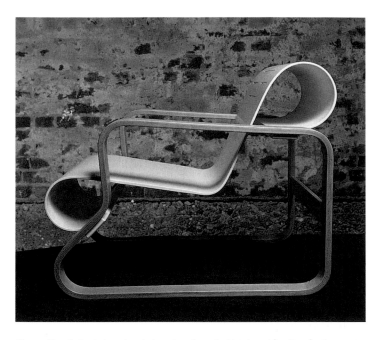

Above: Alvar Aalto designed a whole series of practical bentwood furniture for the sanatorium at Pemar, Finland, from 1921 to1933. The technology was new and attracted well-deserved attention. The furniture is still being produced by Artek.

Below: Aalto had already discovered his characteristic curved shapes by 1929, as shown in these sketches for the Thonet Competition in Berlin. Many of the idioms of the 1960s are already recognisable.

Previous spread: One of the more renowned pupils at Bauhaus was Wilhelm Wagenfelt. He designed amongst other things this series of practical, stackable storage boxes, Kubus, for larders and fridges in 1938.

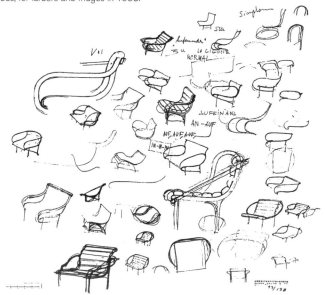

and terraces, but also for new apartment blocks. These had a depth of eight metres instead of the earlier fourteen to fifteen metres, and were called "loaves" because of their narrow shape. The idea was that the flats would have daylight shining through from at least two directions. They were built at Kvarnholmen in Stockholm where many of KF's factories were. HSB (the Tenants' Building Society) and other housing companies throughout the country also adopted the new architecture. Houses were no longer built around closed yards, but placed out in the landscape, parallel to each other.

Garden suburbs further from the inner city were also developed. City inhabitants had been given generous loans as early as the 1910s and 1920s, to allow them the possibility of building their own homes outside the dirty and overcrowded inner city. Enskede, south of Stockholm, is a good example. The overcrowded inhabitants of southern Stockholm could borrow up to 80 percent of the building costs so that they could move out and build themselves a small house with two to three rooms and a kitchen. One condition was that they also did some of the building work themselves, which led to building teams, co-operation and good neighbourliness. The gardens were used to grow potatoes and vegetables. Most people had hens and rabbits, maybe even a pig. The children could grow up in fresh air to become sound, healthy citizens.

The revolutionary Stockholm Exhibition

It was again time for a new résumé, a new exhibition. Gregor Paulsson, director of the Swedish Handcraft Association, and the architect Gunnar Asplund were appointed to direct the work for the Stockholm Exhibition in 1930, which was built up on Djurgården and became known as "the monstrosity". A conflict had already grown up in the planning stage between Gregor Paulsson and the leadership on the one side, and Carl Malmsten, who could not reconcile himself with Functionalism, on the other.

The result was a compromise that also allowed room for arts and crafts. But pure Functionalism dominated, and four million people made a pilgrimage during the summer to the sleek white pavilions with their fluttering flags. They were either delighted or horrified by the New World shown there.

Functionalism was not only presented as a number of new products, but also as a complete social programme. The world stood on the threshold of a new age for a new man. This demanded a completely new attitude to town planning, living and household goods. Industrial products were pitted against craftsmen's products and one of the slogans was: The Utilitarian is the Beautiful. This concept was in the spirit of Le Corbusier: "The house should be like a machine for living in". The Stockholm Exhibition was a watershed between the old and the new; it was now time to prove, once and for all, how much better a utensil was if you peeled away unnecessary decoration. Which, moreover, only made it more expensive.

Since there was still an acute lack of accommodation, many innovative solutions for practical storage were also presented. Chairs were made stackable, beds became sofas in the daytime, or were folded up against the wall like a cupboard. Tables had a practical intermediate height of 60 centimetres and could be used as both dining tables and bedside tables. A lot of the furniture had double functions; bowls, saucepans, glass were all made stackable. Everything was shrewdly devised and easy to move. You could already see the embryo of Swedish standardisation.

Discussions about beautiful and ugly continued in many quarters. Gregor Paulsson did not hesitate to point out: This glass is beautiful, you must use it! This one is ugly, you must reject it! This heated discussion was carried on year in and year out in the magazine Vi (known as Konsumentbladet until 1936). The manifesto *acceptera (accept)* – written in 1931 by Gregor Paulsson, Gunnar Asplund, Walter Gahn, Sven Markelius, Eskil Sundahl and Uno Åhrén – also took up Functionalism's ideas, and propagated for a way of living where one jettisoned the ballast of over-decorated objects, things that were dragged around like pieces of domestic scenery. They criticised objects they considered vulgar and "the masses who were fundamentally conservative, with a view that Industrialism was the natural enemy", but they also carefully sketched out the functions of the New Home, room by room.

The living room was to be a room for Living in, without status furniture. The room should "modestly and pleasantly fulfil its task of serving the whole family". Thus it was important to consider how it was to be furnished already at the drawing-board stage. Doors should not be placed so that the sofa or the extra bed could not fit in. A space for working at home – primarily for the sewing machine – was also important, as was space for storage. The use of the kitchen would be partly eliminated in the future, since gadgets, tinned food and nutrient pills (!) would make food preparation easier. Therefore many houses were built with a secondary kitchen, a small area between the hall and the eating area, where light came through a glass wall between the dining room and the kitchen area. There was room only for one person at a time in these kitchens. It was also claimed that the kitchen was such a dangerous working

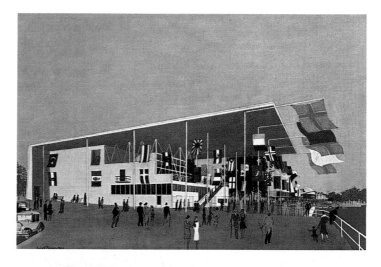

Above: The Stockholm Exhibition in 1930 went down in history as the time and place when Swedes were confronted with Functionalism. It attracted both praise and criticism. Gunnar Asplund was the architect. The picture shows the main entrance to the exhibition.

Left: Several "self-owned-homes" were built up in the exhibition area. These functional terraced houses were designed by Uno Åhrén as an example of good living for the less well-off.

Below: So-called architect's flats were also exhibited in Stockholm. This large, airy drawing room was furnished by Sven Markelius with much of his own furniture and a carpet by Ingegerd Torham.

Above: In 1930, Sven Markelius built his own house in Nockeby using a pure Functionalist style with white surfaces, large windows and terraces. It has an elevated position looking out over the surroundings, the rounded windows of the drawing room resembling the bridge of a ship.

Below: The plan of the second floor of Markelius's house. There is a lot of space for sunshine and fresh air on the large terrace above the drawing room.

Right: This furniture made of plywood and bentwood was designed by Alvar Aalto for the sanatorium at Pemar in 1929–1933. The requirement was that they should be practical, not dust-collectors.

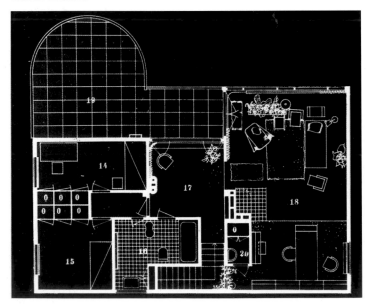

space that children should be kept out! If there wasn't room for them there, this would automatically solve the problem. Even the hall could be largely eliminated in favour of an alcove or similar. "A large hall would immediately become a place to sleep at night," according to the authors. Every apartment, on the other hand, was given a bathroom and some of them the luxury of a balcony.

Wood rather than tubular steel

The new tubular furniture from the continent, so much appreciated by the aesthetic elite, was imported to Sweden during the 1930s by, amongst others, the Tenant Association's housing shop in Stockholm. They were designed by Mies van der Rohe, Marcel Breuer, Le Cobusier – "the engineer of aesthetics" – and his collaborator Charlotte Perriand. This furniture did not meet with great appreciation from the wider public. Since tubular steel, for some reason, was not seen to have "artistic value", it was not covered by any laws of copyright and could be freely copied. For example by A.W. Nilsson's company in Malmö which made exact copies of Mies van der Rohe's elegant – and exceedingly artistic – tubular chair MR 20 with its basket-work seat. But not even this was a bestseller.

No, it was furniture made of wood that counted in Scandinavia. Carl Malmsten was already a famous name and now others appeared, including Bruno Mathsson, Axel Larsson and Josef Frank in Sweden, Alvar Aalto in Finland and Kaare Klint in Denmark. The architects Gunnar Asplund and Sven Markelius also designed furniture, but primarily for their own buildings.

The profession of Furniture Designer originated now, as a result of the special training course at the Tekniska skolan, now Konstfack (the College of Art and Design). Many of those who trained there in the 1930s opened their own businesses or worked for the department store NK, G.A. Berg or Futurum, a young interior design company.

Bruno Mathsson, who was a fifth generation cabinet-maker from Småland, had his own production for all of 50 years. He designed everything from the 1930s–1940s chairs Gräshoppan, Eva and Pernilla, covered in saddle leather, and a fantastic folding-table with a span of 25 to 180 centimetres, to the revolving armchair Jetson and a super-ellipse table (with Piet Hein) in the 1960s. He also studied ergonomics in early years and made functional computer tables in the 1980s. After an inspiring visit to the USA in the early 1950s, Bruno Mathsson designed fifty glass houses with

triple glazing and floor-heating (see page 116). If you could live like that in America, he reasoned, why not in Sweden? Bruno Mathsson was above all an inquisitive person, but also precise and rational. As early as 1934, when his chair Eva came out, he said: "Making a chair should be such an art that sitting in it is not!"

Carl Malmsten had long been a famous name in furniture circles. But in contrast to his colleagues he was a traditionalist and a romantic. The form of the furniture was often subordinated to the well-worked decorations of carved flowers, acanthus scrolls and lion paws. He has gone down in posterity more as an educationalist, perhaps, than a designer. He started Capellagården on Öland, where you can still be taught craftsmanship in the spirit of Carl Malmsten.

The young architect Alvar Aalto in Finland had begun to experiment with bentwood as part of a commission for furnishing the sanatorium at Pemar. Aalto's furniture is today more sought-after than ever, even though one can feel that the chairs made for the sanatorium are rather too low, and perhaps too uncomfortable, for a tall Swede to sit in. But beautiful as sculptures! The covered armchairs, on the other hand, are agreeable to use, especially the ones that rock on a frame of springy wood. No one can deny that Alvar Aalto is the master of bentwood. All the tables, stools, shelves and chairs bear witness to this. This bentwood furniture is still made, more or less by hand, at the Korhonen factory at Åbo.

Aalto and his wife Aino also designed houses and everyday utensils during the 1930s and 1940s. He made the swelling Savoy vase for the Savoy Restaurant in Helsinki. She designed the fluted pressed glass and jugs.

Danish furniture began to make a name for itself in the 1930s and became world-famous in the 1950s. The designer Kaare Klint modernised and recreated old classics above all in the 1930s, through studies of the proportions of the (male!) human body. The 19th century deckchair and the foldable safari chair are associated with him, but in Sweden, however, Klint's fame mainly rested on his beautifully folded paper lamps, the Le Klint lamps. They were cheap to produce and gave soft, pleasant light.

Left: This Functionalist house at Stora Mossen was designed for Gunnar and Alva Myrdal by Sven Markelius in 1937. It is interesting to see how the child evidently "lived" in his play-pen, so that his mother could work in peace.

Above: Gunnar Asplund designed this flat for Sven Wallander and the newly founded HSB. It introduced the secondary kitchen with indirect light from the small dining room, which also served as a bedroom.

Below, left: Gunnar Asplund's leather covered chair for the Swedish Handcraft Association's office at the Stockholm Exhibition in 1930.

The White Houses in Södra Ängby

Södra Ängby, a suburb of Stockholm, has perhaps the world's largest and most uniformly Functionalist housing estate. It was planned in 1933 and designed almost entirely by Edvin Engström. Over 500 houses stand in an undulating park-like area, with unfenced gardens. The rectangular Functionalist forms are emphasized by tall, austere pines in whose dark-green shadows the white-plastered houses with gently sloping roofs stand in rows along gently winding roads. The whole area is now listed and "vandalism", in the form of white sandstone bricks, annexed greenhouses, barred windows and other "quaintnesses" from the 1970s and 1980s, is now prevented. The estate was more or less completed by 1940.

A new generation is now taking over and many of the present owners take particular care to preserve the character of their houses, even indoors. Anna Winter and Tomas Kempe, both architects, were keen to move to Södra Ängby for the sake of these stylistically pure houses. They have lived for nine years in their house, which was built in 1936.

The house, of 160 square metres, was modernised in the 1950s when, amongst other things, they replaced the original simple cornices with more profile d ones. When the Kempe family moved in nine years ago another renovation was carried out, this time of the kitchen. The wall between the maid's bedroom and the tiny kitchen was removed. The new kitchen was given white cupboard doors and modern gadgets. They are now planning yet another conversion, a "functionalisation", as Anna Winter puts it. The white tiles in the kitchen are being replaced by grey mosaic. Plain shelves will be put up, and the left wall of the dining room will be given a round window of the same type that many of the other houses in the area have. Thus the window will not just be aesthetical, but also functional, since it will catch the evening sun.

On the upper floor, however, where three children and two grown-ups must fit in, they have not been entirely true to the

Left: Looking into the living room from the hall. The fabric, Delfinisk rörelse, by Karl Axel Pehrson hangs in the foreground. The left-hand sofa was originally designed by the Celsing office as an overnight sofa for MPs. The right-hand sofa was a bargain from IKEA. Even the coffee table and the long-armed wall lamp are recycled. The carpet by Gunilla Lagerhem-Ullberg and the black armchair by Åke Axelsson are new, while the Thonet chair was made shortly after the turn of the century.

Above: Many houses and flats had open fireplaces in the 1930s. This one is typical. Austere and simple, with a wrought-iron bar and a marble hearth. A contemporary food trolley stands next to the fireplace.

Previous spread: The living room opens out into the dining room. A row of Danish bookcases with glass doors stand along the further wall. They are made from laminated wood and are "Denmark's answer to IKEA's Billy". There are 1960s versions of the Thonet chairs and a food trolley from the 1930s along one wall, and in the middle of the floor a grey-green dining table with Myran chairs round it – a former conference table.

Functionalist spirit of the house. A large hall, for example, has been divided in the middle to make a child's room.

It is difficult to imagine that three children live in the house when you see the austere, Functionalist fittings without the mass of trinkets that usually characterise homes with children. Generous table areas and shiny parquet floors dominate. Large windows let in the autumn sun. On the southern side there is a generous terrace on the ground floor, as well as a long balcony stretching the length of the upper floor.

The furniture is sparse and functional, collected from different periods. Two sofas, one of them a throwaway from the House of Parliament and the other from an IKEA sale, stand on either side of the coffee table inherited from Tomas's father's office, Kempe & Ljunglöf. The Parliament sofa was designed by the Celsing office as an overnight-sofa for members of parliament. The seat can be pulled out at night so that the depth of the bed will be more than that of the sofa. The two drawers under the bed were for the MP's private belongings and bedding. In other words, a very functional piece of furniture.

The large dining table also comes from Kempe & Ljunglöf, where it served as a conference and working table. It has been given a shiny grey-green surface. A row of black Myran chairs stand round the table. Typical Functionalist furniture such as food trolleys, armchairs, lamps, ceramics and posters are placed around the flat. Including a new armchair, designed by Åke Axelsson. The only textiles are Karl Axel Pehrson's black-and-white fabric, Delfinisk rörelse, on the living room wall and Svenskt Tenn's pale yellow elephant-patterned drape in the hall in front of the outdoor clothes. There is a smooth black-and-white carpet, Häggå by Gunilla Lagerhem-Ullberg, under the coffee table.

The lamp over the coffee table, with its long, adjustable arm was found in a refuse container – a typical working-lamp from a photographer's studio or an architect's office. The family think it's perfect. The other lamps have largely been put together from old and new parts.

Above: A small serving-passage has been preserved between the dining room and the kitchen. The door is glazed. The kitchen fittings are white, with light-grey mosaic above the working surface and up to the roof. The oak table is home-made and the chairs are of a rustic, school type.

Right: Functionalist houses are famous for their balconies and terraces. They wanted light and air. This terrace has an autumnal feel, with durable wicker chairs, rustic tables and stools. Privacy is provided by a white canvas awning.

42 Square Metres of Heaven

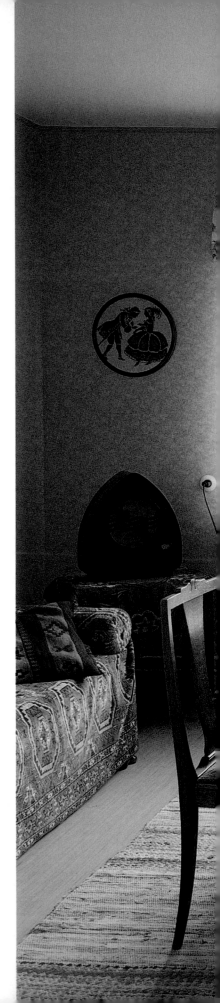

We sometimes dub these 1930s houses, a little contemptuously, "Myrdal houses". By this we mean that economist Gunnar Myrdal and his diplomat wife Alva contributed to the herding together of large, poor families into special housing. The truth was that the Myrdals saw the dire need of many city dwellers. A frightening number of them lived in sheds or small, old-fashioned one-room flats in bad repair. They had no proper kitchens and the toilets were in the yard. It wasn't surprising that the birth rate was the lowest in Europe and that child mortality was high.

The Myrdals wrote their book *Kris i befolkningsfrågan* (*Population Crisis*) in 1934, which lead to the appointment of a social housing enquiry in the following year, and to the subsequent construction of modern, but simple, state-subsidised "large family" houses. You had to have at least three children to qualify for the queue. These new, "large family" houses had central heating, kitchens with stainless steel sinks, hot and cold water, gas cookers and a proper bathroom – although some still insisted that the working classes didn't need the luxury of baths! Refrigerators were, however, considered too expensive.

A kindergarten was attached to most of the "large family" houses – a kind of nursery or play-school. The buildings were narrow, like lamella, standing unattached in green surroundings.

A flat has been preserved in one of these houses, at Stickelbärsvägen 7 in Stockholm, and turned into a museum under the administration of the City Museum.

The Jonasson family – father Sven-Simon, a plumber, mother Anna, a cleaner, and four teenage sons – once lived here. They moved in on October 1st 1937 and thought that 42 square metres was pure heaven. Hot water came from the bathroom tap, and by putting a token in the gas-meter you immediately got heat in the cooker. There was an extendable marble slab for baking, and a Reda shelf with glass jars for dry foodstuffs. The dining area was divided

and had a kitchen sofa in which the twin boys could sleep at night. The other two sons shared the small room, where one of them had a bed and the other slept in a "concertina" fold-away bed. The parents slept in the living room, in an ottoman that became a sofa during the day. The living room was also the "best room", off-limits to the boys when their father was at home. When he was away, however, things were different. Apparently, they even played ping-pong on the big table in the middle of the room. All clothing was stored in two cupboards.

It has not been entirely easy to re-create the original 1937 furnishings in this flat. Birgit Burström (from Handtryckta tapeter) found the wallpaper in a country shop in Southern Sweden, and the linoleum comes from Germany – where the old factory proved to be still operating. Door handles, switches, cupboard doors, furniture and utensils have been collected from neighbours, children and relatives.

Left: This kitchen was modern in the 1930s and had a black gas cooker with an oven, a stainless-steel sink and a lot of cupboards. A modern Reda shelf is mounted above the sink, storing peas, beans, flour and macaroni.

Above, left: The dining area is somewhat separate from the kitchen, and also serves as sleeping space for two. The marble slab for baking is on the left in the kitchen.

Above, right: The luxurious bathroom has windows, a bathtub, a toilet and a hand basin. Washing was done both in the bathtub and in the communal laundry in the cellar.

Previous spread: The table stands right in the middle of the living room, or "best room". The furniture is standard with no particular character. There is a gramophone on the sideboard next to mother's sewing and darning corner. Four sons provided her with a lot of work. The parents slept in the sofa/ottoman.

Josef Frank's Villa in Falsterbo

Josef Frank came to Sweden from wartime Vienna with his Swedish wife in 1933. He had already designed many houses and villas in Austria and abroad, and also for the Paris Exhibition of 1925.

He was neither a modernist nor a traditionalist, but adopted a kind of Anglo-Saxon common-sense view. He also removed architecture from its conventionally elevated position to a practical every-day level by asking: "Which shape does the hall have? How do you reach the different rooms? How does the sitting area relate to the windows and doors? These questions must be answered and the house itself consists of these elements. That is what I call modern architecture!"

Externally, his houses follow the Functionalist tradition, with clean lines and many balconies, patios and roof-terraces. But internally he shocks the Swedish public, brought up on the Swedish Handcraft Association's utilitarian norms. Josef Frank makes wild use of patterns, with floral cretonnes on his sofas and curtains. He makes his sofas almost immorally deep and has cocktail cabinets with leopard rugs in front of them. Is this a provocation or a manifestation of his continental view of the home? Frank also claims that a plurality of patterns benefits a room. Together they create tranquility.

During his time at the Svenskt Tenn company, where Estrid Ericson engaged him after his arrival in Sweden, he designed a host of patterns. Of these, about 125 have been printed on linen and cotton fabrics. Josef Frank also designed sofas, chairs and tables for Svenskt Tenn.

Before he moved to Sweden, Josef Frank had spent his summers at Falsterbo. There are five summerhouses here, designed by him during 1927–1936. The first, and maybe the most important, is Villa Wethje, designed for the industrialist Walter Wethje from Malmö. The basic shape of the house is irregular; giving the impression of a small number of houses collected round three yards. They do, in fact,

Left: The original pink plaster walls were covered in the 1970s with fashionable white aluminium panels. From a distance, however, this looks like wood panelling. We can also see one of the round hall windows.

Above: The twin doors of the living room can be opened onto the Japanese garden and the middle yard, thus connecting outside with inside. Some of the garden furniture was designed by Josef Frank. Inside there is a glimpse of Alvar Aalto's handsome serving trolley.

Previous spread:
Villa Wethje was built to Josef Frank's design in 1936. Its random shape sets it apart from the other houses at Falsterbo. The house encloses some tall pine trees that he wanted to save.

have a U-shape, broken up by rounded walls, unexpected angles and windows and terraces on different levels. You approach the house via a middle garden, where space has been kept for existing tall pine trees, giving the place a Southern European character.

Inside the door of the small, but striking, hall with its huge round window, the house divides into one part for sleeping and one part for socialising. There is a "Japanese garden" outside the large bedroom. There are twin doors of glass on both sides, and when they are open you have the feeling of sitting out in the open. From the large lower hall with its two-storied windows, you enter the upper lounge, which also leads out to the famous Frank terraces. From here you had a view of the sea – before the trees grew too high.

Concerning the random planning of this house, Josef Frank describes his thoughts on rooms thus: "The right-angled room is the least suitable in which to live; it is very practical as a furniture warehouse, but of little use for anything else. I believe, that if you draw a polygon at random, with right-angles and obtuse angles, it will be more suitable as a plan for a room than the regular right-angled one."

Anna-Brita Hedberg now lives in Villa Wethje. She bought the house with her husband in 1946. The façade had pink plaster at that time but was subsequently painted with white plastic paint, which flaked and fell off. Today it is covered with white American aluminium panelling which, according to Anna-Brita Hedberg, is the best they have had.

A lot of the furniture has been changed and moved during the years, but Anna-Brita remembers when Mr. Frank himself came to "inspect", shortly after the family had moved in. He had nothing to remark on as far as she can remember. The dining room furniture is still intact, including a table for 22 people complete with slender, cane-seated chairs. The curved sofa on the upper floor, the stools in the hall and some of the garden furniture are also the work of Josef Frank.

Right: You are met in the hall by the large round window, which captures the trees in the back yard like a picture frame. The floor is laid with large black-and-white tiles, and the furniture consists of an austere black marble bench on a brass stand.

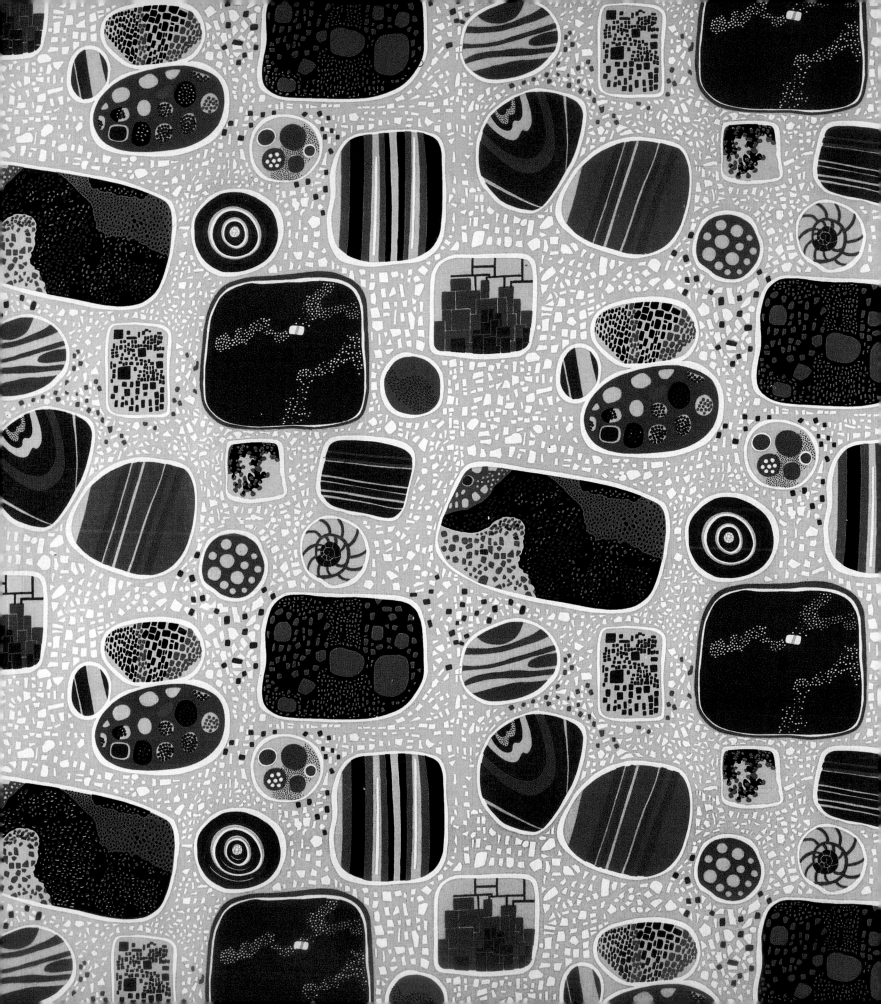

Left: Josef Frank is probably best known for his textile patterns that are still sold by Svenskt Tenn in Stockholm. The pattern here is called Terrazzo.

Above: The open dining room with its large windows still has furniture by Josef Frank, including the dining table and the light chairs with cane seats. Some of them have been repaired, after children's inquisitive fingers picked holes in the cane-work.

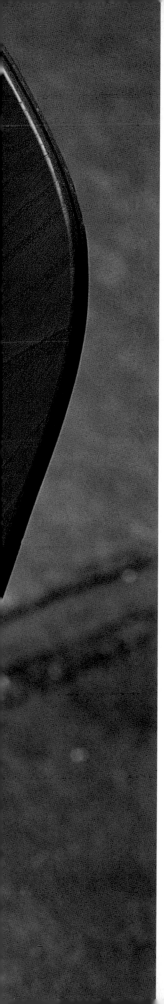

The 1940s

Overshadowed by war

Functionalism has planed out. The socially-orientated train of thought is still there, and will be strengthened during the coming decades, but the austere interiors and strict tubular steel furniture are not bought by many people.

Swedish Design, in its new, modified and less austere form, does however receive great appreciation at the World Exhibition in New York in 1939, where they talk lyrically about Swedish Modern, which was also the name of the Swedish pavilion. Estrid Ericson and Josef Frank's room Studio, and Astrid Sampe and Elias Svedberg's weekend cottage interior for the NK department store were the most talked-about. This was something new, both for the Americans and for international visitors. The rounded, but functional, forms of the furniture, stripped of all unnecessary frippery, and the flexible furnishings and beautiful textiles filled the viewers with surprise and joy. It was both new and deeply traditional.

Furniture manufacture in Sweden now enters a phase of greater standardisation and industrial production. Not only do they make furniture for the wealthy but also, very consciously, for the people who are slowly but surely climbing up the prosperity ladder. Those who get larger flats and thereby room for better storage, wider beds, proper dining tables and coffee tables, and more space for the children.

An optimistic belief in the Good Society begins to grow after the end of the War in 1945. Now everything will get better – housing, food, spare time. Shabby things will soon just be a memory. One can even accept simple, mass-produced furniture as practical, without seeing it as a sign of nondescript poverty. The Swedish Welfare State now begins to take shape.

What did this renowned New Identity look like, exactly? The young interior designer Lena Larsson could describe it, having done

Above: Like Alvar Aalto, Bruno Mathsson did a lot of work with bentwood. This is Mathsson's reclining chair Pernilla, covered in sheepskin. Manufactured in 1944.

Below: It was almost obligatory that upper class homes were furnished with furniture from Carl Malmsten's company. This picture shows the bishop's residence in Västerås. Carl and Siv Malmsten visited it to insure that everything was properly arranged.

Previous spread: The Americans Charles and Ray Eames designed a lot of furniture in the 1940s, some of it with Eero Saarinen from Finland, using bentwood. This chair of moulded birch was designed by Charles Eames in 1946.

a study of more than 200 Swedish homes. With an unerring feel for standardisation, homes were furnished in the same way irrespective of how many family members there were to share the flat. There was a sofa in the middle of the longest wall in the "best room" with an ornamental clock over it, a coffee table and some armchairs grouped around it, knick-knacks everywhere. Children were of course "prohibited". And there were places to sleep everywhere, but seldom in the "best room". This meant that everything had to take place in the kitchen, which was often minimal. This was where the baking, mending, washing-up and cleaning was done, from morning to night, by the housewife, when she took out everything that needed to be patched and sewn. The children also did their homework here, and somebody always slept in the kitchen at night.

A long and animated debate was carried on in the magazine Vi, about living standards and the responsibility of politicians to provide better housing. The Myrdals' book had prompted a social housing inquiry. KF's architectural office and the public housing sector started the building of subsidised housing, consisting of larger flats with two or three rooms and large kitchens. Åke Huldt of the Swedish Handcraft Association (now Swedish Design) was in charge of the newly started Home Standard courses. Lena Larsson held courses arranged by the NKI school, about the furnishing of the home and what was necessary and unnecessary. Artur Hald, Åke Huldt, Edna Martin and Elias Svedberg wrote the course literature.

Now people were to be taught, in the era of post-war scarcity, to use their imagination at a time when there were neither money nor products. For example, by taking away the ends of the beds and placing them at an angle in the living room, a pleasant, daytime sitting area could be created. Or by buying the same kind of chairs for the whole flat, so that they could be used both as dining chairs, and chairs for the coffee table and the desk. A Swedish version of the Windsor chair was considered the best. Another trick was to opt for folding tables instead of large, space-consuming dining tables. Mixing old and new. Making bunk beds for the children. And so on.

The first, modern basic furniture, "knocked-down" furniture that one put together at home, now began to appear. Elias Svedberg and Lena Larsson designed the Triva series and NK sold them. NK opened its Living department just two years later in 1947, with Lena Larsson in charge. This was something new, for they often changed the window displays in unexpected ways. Textiles, light furniture – safari chairs and wicker furniture – and functional utensils were displayed in an enticing way. People made a pilgrimage to the shop.

Even KF (the Co-operative Society) was active. They manufactured their own light chairs and tables, cupboards and the child's bed Tripp–trapp-trull. Production was in Lammhult and the furniture was delivered directly to the customer to keep prices down. The department store PUB had only display items.

The decade of measurement

There were many good intentions in this, the decade of the family and of reconstruction. One wanted to raise things up to the ideal. But first one had to establish what was wrong. So it became the decade of measurement. The Institute of Home Research was founded and Brita Åkerman and Carin Boalt busily started weighing and measuring. With their tape measures, they followed housewives and discovered that they walked seven kilometres a day in their homes! This needed rationalisation! The kitchen was re-designed so that larder, taps and cooker were closer together. The china cupboard was placed above the sink and the cupboard for saucepans next to the cooker. A workbench next to the cooker was also seen as necessary. Working surfaces were raised to 80 centimetres.

Measurements for beds, chairs, tables were standardised – how high, how wide, how close to the wall to be able to get past? How many cupboards and wardrobes were needed? How were things stored? How was the washing-up done, where was it placed? How was the shopping done? The fridge became a necessity. The kitchen area increased from six square metres to ten or more, and home loans were increased from 1000 to 2000 Crowns.

The standardisation of the 1940s is still the basis of much of our modern housing.

Organic Modernism

Despite the fact that the 1940s was a "Swedish" decade, amiable, but perhaps with a paucity of design, due to wartime isolation and a lack of materials, we still got some inspiration from abroad. Not least the pliable bentwood and plywood furniture proved very suitable. It was a kind of organic Modernism, represented by Alvar Aalto who was already well-known, and by Ray and Charles Eames from the USA, who manufactured interesting furniture using moulded plywood.

The bentwood technique that Alvar Aalto had patented in 1933 was fairly manual and therefore time-consuming. The solution came, as often before, from an unexpected area. It was the experiments done by the aircraft industry in its search for strong, new materials that gave the furniture industry machine-pressed, glued plywood. Now stackable chairs, shelves and cupboards could be mass-produced at much lower prices.

Left: This chair, Cattelin, from Gemla Möbler, was designed in 1948 from an old 19th century prototype. It was commissioned by the Cattelin Restaurant in Stockholm. Now it is one of Gemla's classics.

Below: Homes were cramped in the 1930s and 1940s. All space-saving ideas were welcome. This flat, with tip-up beds, was shown at the Stockholm Exhibition by Sven Wallander, HSB. The furniture came from the Tenant Association's furniture shop's design office.

Bottom: The ideal family. A photo from Riksbanken (Bank of Sweden) and the Swedish Handcraft Association's house furnishing catalogue, with information and propaganda for clean, functional and airy Swedish homes.

The Summer Home

Yearning for the country – a very Swedish phenomenon

Even middle-class Swedes began to have a double life in the 1930s and 40s. People were in the country in the summer, and the rest of the year in their town flat. The upper classes had always lived this way, and even country dwellers often still had a large winter house and a simpler summer house.

To begin with this was a rather amusing migration, triggered basically by a dream of Nature and a return to the simple life – that is to say, to similary primitive conditions people had just left behind them in their town life, but there in the form of a flat with no modern facilities! The summer cottage was a manifestation that people now could afford to do more in their holidays than just bicycle camping. It was, moreover, a re-connection to their roots and to the Swedish soil that most people came from. The need to build and to do-it-yourself. To garden. To give the children fresh air. And maybe the most important of all – to own, in contrast to renting a flat.

The Sports Cottage at Årsta

At the inland sea resort of Årsta, 40 kilometres south of Stockholm, one of the first planned weekend cottage areas was built at the start of the 1930s. The initiative came from the founder and head of HSB (Tenants' Building Society), Sven Wallander, and was a large experiment: "A leisure area for ordinary people". They were called "sports cottages" and were about fifteen to twenty five square metres and were partly self-built on leasehold plots. These leases were so low (14 öre per square metre annually) and life-long with hereditary rights, that it now costs more to collect the sum than to receive it. Therefore almost all the 800 houses have been sold to their leaseholders.

There was also, in the area closest to the sea, a hotel with a restaurant, a square with shops, and small "hardboard tents" for those who could not afford their own houses. Water was fetched from a tap on the boundary of each plot, slops were emptied in a hole in the ground and there was a dry privy on each site.

The first weekend cottage was built in 1929. It has now been converted to a museum, thanks to the enthusiast Richard Roosvall. The cottage is intact and furnished with 1930s objects from the area. This cottage was not modernised and extended, like most others, due to the fact that it was owned by the newspaper Dagens Nyheter which rented it out to employees. Therefore there was no one who looked after it.

The small fifteen square metre cottage: Model 5 – the most sold kind – was furnished and opened in the spring of 1999.

"People in the area have been very generous," says Richard Roosvall. "People have come by almost every day with things they have found that could be suitable. I am most pleased with the little black wood stove with two hotplates".

The weekend cottage at Årsta has yellow-painted panelling and white window frames. There are a table, bench and two chairs on the covered veranda. The single room has a sofa-bed, some chairs

Left: The small stove doesn't invite large-scale cooking, but meals were presumably simpler in the summer. The kitchen area in the corner is not yet complete; the stovepipe is missing. Water was fetched at the boundary of the plot, and slops thrown into a hole in the ground!

Above, left: The kitchen panelling is a beautiful pale-green, in nice contrast to the blue sideboard. Paraffin lamps were used, because there was no electricity.

Above, right: The single room is panelled with plain pinewood, which has darkened with time. The furniture consists of a sofa, a table and some chairs, one of which could serve as a bed. But there is also a wind-up gramophone and a bookshelf. Culture also played its part!

Previous spread: The weekend cottage from the Årsta sea resort is one of 800 built in the 1930s, and is preserved today as a museum. The newly painted, fifteen square metre house stands on a plot quite close to the square. The other cottages have undergone many changes and modernisation over time.

and a wide armchair of the sort common in the crowded 1930s: constructed as a bed that could be unfolded at night, with room for two small children.

The kitchen equipment is so primitive that it is almost impossible to understand how a housewife could prepare food for several people daily. The stove stands by itself with nowhere to place things. Nor is there any working surface. But there is, on the other hand, a pantry with a window. However, people probably didn't prepare the same complicated meals as in town. And there was a restaurant in the area.

Rebuilding an "Old Hovel"

"A squalid little shack on concrete plinths, that's what we'd bought," says Maria Lomholt of the wooden, blue-grey house behind a high palisade of pine stakes – a kind of fencing typical for Falsterbo.

Today it is difficult to imagine the small, neglected house in a sea of brambles – " a hovel ready for demolition" according to the bank, unwilling to make a loan – when one now sees the low, child-friendly house, with children running in and out of the spacious garden.

That's often the way it is with weekend cottages. Especially those built during, or at the end of, the war when materials were hard to come by. The original enthusiasts lost interest or grew too old or too ill to look after their houses any longer. Dilapidation came as quickly as the weeds.

This particular summer house was built in the sand dunes at Falsterbo sometime during the 1940s. It is one of the first modular houses to be constructed and has an outer wall used as a frame around the floor that was laid later. The inner walls were placed on the floor, which made it easy to take them down and redistribute the interior of the house, explains Maria Lomholt, who has done a lot of the work herself, with her husband Per Nimér.

They opened the house both upwards and inwards, making it into a single room with a built-in glazed veranda on one side. They made space for a bathroom and two sleeping galleys behind the narrow, but practical, kitchen. Everything was painted white to give an impression of cleanliness and space. The floors are old, but have been sanded and treated with lye and soap to give them a pleasant pale hue.

"It was a bit sensitive, considering all the sand that the kids and the dogs bring in. But we open all the doors and sweep it straight out, if it doesn't blow out by itself!"

It is honourable, both for an old house and its new owners, to make such a transformation from decay to robust health.

Left: The parents' small bedroom has white wooden panelling and a soap-treated floor. Two Hästen beds with light down pillows promise a good night's sleep. There is a rough linen curtain in front of the wardrobe, replacing doors.

Above, left: The children's bedroom only has room for the bunk beds. Even this room is painted white and has blue-and-white bedding. Everything is as functional as possible.

Above, right: The tiny shower and washing room is a dream in white, with a wooden floor, an IKEA sink and customised radiators.

Previous spread, left: Most of the 80 square metres are taken up by the living room, which is refreshingly uncluttered by furniture, suitable as a playground for both their own and other children. There are bouncy cushions, a wide Danish sofa and gymnastic rings as well as a soft carpet to lie on. A raffia-covered stool by Josef Frank stands on the carpet.

Previous spread, right: A simple, sacral, whitewashed open fireplace with an untreated cement chimney shaft has been built into the wall opposite the kitchen. The walls are of smooth, white-painted wood panelling.

Above: The blue-grey 1940s house is surrounded by green trees – compensating for the grass that will not grow on the sandy ground. But it will, insist the owners, who have had the house for only five years.

Right: The house opens onto the built-in veranda, which also serves as an entrance from the garden. It is used as a combined dining room and living room, with a long table where all sorts of activities can take place at the same time. It is covered with a tablecloth by Gunnel Sahlin. The 1940s chairs are from Nässjö chair factory.

Modern Life in an 18th Century House

Many people dream of a genuine, old house as their weekend home. One that has character, solid workmanship and a well-established garden. There are plenty of such houses in Sweden. Louise Hallin and Anders Palmér found a whitewashed house with a tiled roof and blue window frames on Gotland in 1990. It had gone into a quiet slumber of dilapidation. A ruined kitchen bore witness to the 18th century, after which several people have owned the property. Finally, in the 1930s, it was inhabited by a man who cooked his food on a trivet.

"It was almost inevitable," relates Louise Hallin, "that we should preserve as much as possible of the old, making only careful changes and letting the house continue its life without artificiality."

So they installed electricity and water, but left the bottom floor intact with its original floor of solid heartwood planks and white-washed walls. The new windows were based on the original ones. The old collapsed kitchen door, facing the sea and the sunset, was transformed into a glass porch leading out to the sitting area that Anders Palmér built with stone from the ruined kitchen. A new kitchen was installed in an adjoining room. The unfitted attic was, however, insulated in the modern way and had its windows made

Left and above, right: The living room is a vibrating ultramarine, and the old floor of solid heartwood planks is intact. The house has slightly angled window niches typical of Gotland, to reflect the light into the room. The furniture is a mixture of finds at auctions and newly-bought Gustavian furniture from IKEA.

Above, left: At the back of the house, where there used to be a kitchen and a bakery, there is now a wonderful sitting area that catches the evening sun. Anders Palmér has built this from the fallen stone of the old kitchen. The porch has been given a glass door with an aluminium frame.

Previous spread: This is many people's dream of a summerhouse! This whitewashed Gotland house with its pan-tiled roof and pale blue window frames and doors looks today, after a long renovation, like it did when built the end of the 18th century.

draughtproof. A shower and a toilet were installed. The house was to be lived in, even during the winter.

Houses on Gotland often surprise us with their daring colour combinations. One example is Taksten's House nearby, where the local government has helped in researching the original colours from the 18th and 19th centuries. It is now a museum and Louise Hallin has found inspiration for her own house there. Thus, one enters the house through a hall painted in dark terracotta. She has fixed the whitewash with egg tempera in the old way. The living room is also whitewashed, but has an intensive ultramarine colour. Thanks to the vibrating light on Gotland, which shines in through

Above: The upper floor has one large and two small bedrooms. The limestone gables are untreated, while the floorboards have been painted white. The sea or the sunset can be seen through a large window from the bed or the comfortable armchairs. A large sheepskin rug lies on the grey floor.

Right: The small room between the gable rooms has been made into a kitchen with a modern cooker and a large French porcelain sink, which also serves as "the everyday china cupboard"! Open shelving, with or without curtains, and a narrow built-in pantry add to the continental atmosphere. The walls are spatter-painted with glue-paint.

four windows, the room does not have a cold feel, rather the opposite. The colour spreads warmth and pleasure!

The easy way to decorate a wall in the old days was to spatter-paint. This method used relatively little paint and gave an exciting, living result. This method succeeds best using glue paint; its turgid consistency meant that only one coat was necessary. When it had dried, a couple of different colours were spattered to create a "pattern". Louise Hallin has painted her light-green kitchen with patterns of white and black using this splatter method. The open kitchen is otherwise a mixture of the genuine Swedish, French esprit and modern simplicity – a style that seems to suit the family well.

The Black House in the Meadow

As his final-year project at KTH's (Royal Technical College) architecture degree-course in 1998, Daniel Snidare chose to design a weekend house and build it himself. It was a hands-on method of following an idea from inception, via paper and CAD-designs, to completed building. It also sprang from a need that his own family had.

The site was measured out on a relatively windy field at Hide on northern Gotland. Corners that were sheltered from the wind had to be created. The open field was to be planted with trees to create a more park-like area. The house, which came to consist of several parts with irregular forms, was constructed to provide "sun-corners" for morning, mid-day and evening light.

Since the whole point of a weekend cottage, according to Daniel, is "leisure" and "lazing", they left the field in its natural state as a flower meadow – thus eliminating grass mowing. The parts of the house were connected on the south side by a 100 square metre wooden deck. A 60 square metre eating and sitting area of Gotland limestone, cut up on site, was laid in the evening corner.

All the materials in the house are local, as far as possible. A neighbouring farmer has provided timber, the wooden decking comes from a nearby saw-mill and the specially designed windows in three different sizes from a local carpentry. The house is painted black with a mixture of linseed oil and iron oxide pigment; paint which is both good, inexpensive and environment-friendly. The same applies to the treatment of the deck, which is done with so-called Roslag's mahogany, a mixture of linseed oil, turpentine and tar. All the windows and woodwork are painted in differing shades of grey.

Daniel Snidare has done the welding himself and has treated the

many cast-iron details with linseed oil. These features, including window benches, the kitchen shelving and a ladder to the sleeping-loft give the house its character. Even some of the garden furniture and indoor cupboards are his own design.

The three-part house with its outhouse and earth cellar, looks light and airy out on the green meadow, despite its black colour. The angles conjoin harmoniously and the dark-grey rafters are decorative elements bearing aloft the gently sloping pentroofs. The tall windows and doors on the south side provide a studio atmosphere, and from the inside – the living room – you can easily look out across the decking and the whole meadow to the edge of the woods beyond.

The two bedrooms are at opposite ends, since the house is used by sibling families, while the central part is shared. There are three exits – directly onto the deck on the south side, onto the evening corner with its limestone paving and out eastwards through the terracotta-red hallway. The floor is laid with oiled-cork tiling. The kitchen is at one end of the living room, opening out towards the seating area next to the open brick fireplace. The wardrobes, the sofa in the large room and many other details are built on-site and are quietly and cleverly integrated in the room.

The ready-made furniture also connects to the timeless, ecological thinking behind the house. The dining table and another small table come from Norrgavel, designed by Nirvan Richter, and the chairs are by Arne Jacobsen and Bruno Mathsson.

Above, left: In the morning corner, between the entrance and the fence, you are sheltered from the wind. The door leads to the terracotta-red hall and through to the main room beside the large bedroom. One small bedroom has its own door to the deck, to the left of the hall door. The table was made by Daniel Snidare from his own design.

Right: The tall windows and door open onto the deck, which begins to warm up in the early spring. Tomatoes thrive. If it gets too light indoors, the thin linen curtains can be drawn. The deck is treated with so-called Roslag's mahogany and the classical furniture is from Grythyttan.

Previous spread: This sheltered corner captures the evening sun. It has pale limestone paving which is pleasantly cooling on really hot days. The outdoor furniture has the same grey colour as the indoor woodwork. The door leads to the main room and the kitchen.

Left: There are few right-angles in the light and airy main room, which has several exits and sitting places. The walled stove has a narrow, English cast-iron stovepipe and the floor is laid with oiled-cork tiles. The sofas are built-in, but the other furniture is flexible and easy to move.

Above: A close-up of the working surface and shelving in the kitchen. The narrow oak shelf in the middle of the mosaic wall is practical for herbs, mugs and other things you want to keep handy. The cast-iron brackets and windowsill have been made by Daniel Snidare himself.

The 1950s

The idea of design is developed

The 1950s have been called the decade of design. The war is over. Money starts coming in and living standards rise. There are free meals at school. Self-service shops, charter travel and TV all make their arrival.

The big change came with TV, which brought with it a new way of living and furnishing. It was the icon that was put in the centre, with the sofa and armchairs all pointed towards the set, instead of towards each other for conversation. The "TV thermos" made it possible to drink hot coffee while the programme was on. There were also supper plates and cutlery, designed in an economical, flexible way suitable for casual meals at the coffee table. The party fork was created by Pierre Forsell at Gense, the TV-pot Signatur by Carl-Arne Breger, and all the decorated cups and plates for the new way of entertaining by Stig Lindberg.

Thanks to the TV and the invention of foam rubber, modern upholstered furniture was created. Foam rubber stuffing made comfort quite cheap, superseding down-filled furniture. Soft sitting was necessary since you sat in front of the TV for a long time. This gave an upswing for a new kind of furniture in an industry that otherwise continued to work with quite traditional wooden furniture. Everything that came to personify "the design-happy fifties" was created, above all, in utility design – textiles, glass and chinaware.

Astrid Sampe, the textile artist, was in charge of NK's Textilkammare (textiles department). She created new and exquisite patterns for curtains and fabrics, amongst other things, working with Viola Gråsten. There was much to catch up on after the unobtrusive 1940s. Astrid Sampe and NK presented the exhibition Signerad textil (Signed Textiles) in 1954, with textiles designed by herself, Viola Gråsten, Karl Axel Pehrson, Stig Lindberg, Olle

Baertling, Alvar Aalto, Sven Markelius, Anders Beckman and other famous architects and artists. Success! The exhibition Linnelinjen (the Linen Line) came the next year, with table linen and bed linen in strong colours. This was also a success and a fresh approach to bedding in general.

The dynamic Stig Lindberg was now the artistic leader at Gustavsberg's factories. Patterns and designs flowed from his hand. Spisa ribb, the brown-striped dinner service, and the ovenproof Terma, with its revolutionary triangular frying pan, are amongst his best known work. Hertha Bengtson made the dinner service Blå eld for Rörstrand and Sigurd Persson designed practical, deep stainless steel dishes with lids and cutlery, Servus, for KF. Sven Palmqvist became famous for his Fuga, centrifuged bowls , and the young Erik Höglund for rustic glasses with a blistered surface. Kaj Frank in Finland designed simple, functional glasses and chinaware for Notsjö and Arabia; real best sellers today.

The designer became an appreciated and important cog in the production process during the 1950s. New design and quality became prestigious in the growing prosperity of the post-war years. People also spoke about the quality of the buyer and not just the quality of what he bought.

This design was aimed at young people. They sat in bat armchairs. ("Ugly and degenerate" according to smug adults.) Thus it became to be an important watershed between new and old ages of furnishing. They put their books (if they could afford any) in a flexible wall bookcase by Nisse Strinning and put one of Viola Gråsten's long-pile rugs on the floor. They bought kidney-shaped teak or jacaranda veneer tables and papered the contrast wall with abstract patterns of grey, black, white and yellow.

The Danish furniture industry was already world-famous and supplied us with well-made teak furniture, lightly upholstered and often covered with a grey or brown woollen cloth. The reason for the success of Danish furniture was partly its modernity – it was light and low, with organic shapes – partly because it was functional and excellently crafted. That Danish craftsmanship was so high was due in part to the annual exhibition shows at the Danska Snedkerlauget (Joinery Group) that nurtured the demand for, and interest in, well-made furniture. A chair by Hans Wegner was elected "the world's most beautiful chair" in 1951 after a vote at the Museum of Modern Art in New York. It was christened The Round Chair, a bar in Chicago ordered 400 and set the ball rolling.

Börge Mogensen, Finn Juhl and Arne Jacobsen are other well-known Danish stars of the furniture business. Arne Jacobsen's three-

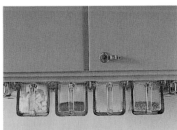

Above: The Dane Arne Jacobsen designed this light swivel armchair, Svanen, for the SAS hotel in Copenhagen. A more enclosing version was called Ägget.

Left: The practical Reda shelves with glass holders for groceries could be found in almost every 1950s home, in a row under the kitchen wall-cupboard.

Left: The armchair, Lamino, was designed in 1956 by Yngve Ekström for Swedese and was chosen as the piece of furniture of the century, in 2000. These are newly produced versions, covered with sheepskin.

Previous spread: Swedish textile became world-famous in the 1950s, not least due to "ambassador" Astrid Sampe at NK's Textilkammare (textiles department). The fabric in this picture, Pythagoras, was designed by Sven Markelius for a curtain in Linköping's civic hall. It was printed by Ljungbergs in Floda.

Look page 96

Picture bottom left.

Arm chair Lamino
designed 1956 by
Yngve Ekström
Vaggeryd Småland.

I bought our chairs
~~1957 our~~ 1957 probbly
at NK and had them
shipped to Kisumi
Backcover tea cup on
pilaster shelf.

legged chair Myran came out in 1952 and is to be found today in every discerning home. Later a safer, four-legged version was produced. The upholstered armchairs, Svanen and Ägget, were designed by Jacobsen for the SAS-hotel at Copenhagen in 1958. They had a form-moulded frame of fibreglass, an exciting new material. These chairs fetch high prices at auctions today, especially if they are covered with leather and come from the hotel itself, where the furnishings were recently sold.

Lena Larsson discovers the living room

The H55 exhibition took place on the pier, Parapeten, at Helsingborg in 1955. It became a manifestation of everything new and designed; for the new age, the new life and the new materials.

The interior designer Lena Larsson furnished a house called Skal och Kärna (Shell and Kernel), designed by Mårten Larsson/Anders William-Olsson, where children were the prime movers. The house was dominated by a living room with a climbing-tree in the middle and a day-bed for play and story time along one wall. There was a system of shelves and cupboards attached to a large table with room for all sorts of activities. It was a long way from the heavy dining table with its trimmings. And a long way from the conventional, closed "best" room. Instead they had furnished a small room for the adults, and for music, next to the bedroom.

This, of course, created much discussion. Were children to take over everything?! Many felt that it was like living in the middle of a spring-clean, while others saw a return to the old, large country kitchens where everyone could work and be together at the same time. This idea was strengthened by the plain birch and pine furniture, such as Windsor-style chairs, gate-leg tables and open shelving. Proper children's furniture was born. The bunk bed Kulan and Växa-med-läxa, bought as a kit, were sold by KF at the end of the 1950s.

These modern and practical ideas for living continued to be developed in the magazine Allt i Hemmet, where Lena Larsson was the technical editor, and in the magazine Vi's supplement "Vi husmödrar". This was published for several years and illuminated the home from all aspects, from the idea of Beauty to the measurements of beds and how to equip kitchen cupboards. Some of it was thought provoking, some of it was lecturing. But they meant so well, in this the decade of continued standardisation!

Since the lack of housing was still catastrophic, house construction increased. People cried out for larger and lighter flats. The

Above: The very latest in Swedish design was displayed at the H55 Exhibition in Helsingborg. A strict, lined fabric by Astrid Sampe is shown here with Sigurd Persson's practical stainless steel dishes with lids.

Left: Alf Svensson constructed the armchair, Contour, for H55. It was manufactured by Dux, with thin upholstery nd a lacquered tubular steel frame.

Below: More H55. Lena Larsson furnished the exhibition house Skal och Kärna (Shell and Kernel), transforming the best room into a communal room with a climbing-tree right in the middle. Many people found this sloppy and shocking. The watercolour is by Lena Larsson.

architects Backström & Reinius designed the famous terrace houses that climb on top of each other in Gröndal outside Stockholm.

The modern suburb was born in the 1950s with the inauguration of the ABC suburb of Vällingby, outside Stockholm. A for Arbete (Work), B for Bostad (Home), C for Centrum (Centre). The idea was that you could live and work here without having to leave the suburb. And it certainly worked. The centre was built with the civic hall, Trappan, the cinema, Fontänen, the department store, Kvickly, small shops, a post office and chemists. Detached slices and blocks of flats were grouped around the centre, with terraced and semi-detached housing further out. The ideal society had been created!

Vällingby has recently been renovated, after a period of decline, in conjunction with its 40th jubilee, and again functions well as a suburb.

Above: Stig Lindberg was Gustavsberg's diligent artistic leader for many years. His dinner service, Spisa ribb, was a formidable best seller. The kitchen linen is by Marianne Nilsson, Almedahls.

Left: Charles Eames created this light armchair from moulded polyether with legs of wood and metal in 1950.

Below: IKEA opened its first furniture store in Älmhult in 1958. Founder Ingvar Kamprad had already been selling furniture directly from factory to customer. This is one of the first furnished showrooms. It had contrast wallpaper, teak furniture with black details, TV and TV-thermos.

Above: The 1950s was the decade of signed textiles. Astrid Sampe put on an exhibition at NK in 1954 with the same name, Signerad textil. This is a black-and-white printed fabric, Delfinisk rörelse, by Karl Axel Pehrson, produced by Ljungbergs in Floda.

Right: Arne Jacobsen's Myran can be called the chair of chairs. It was made of pressed plywood with thin metal legs, three in the first version of 1952, four in the later, more stable models.

Two-room Flats from the 1950s

Some typical 1950s flats have been re-created, both in the modern ABC suburb Vällingby and the small village of Hällefors in Bergslagen, as exhibitions of a lost era. The one in Vällingby was a temporary exhibit for the suburb's 40th jubilee, while Hällefors has invested in permanent exhibition flats in a lamella house built in the 1950s at the centre of the village.

The 52 square metre flat in Vällingby with its bathroom and balcony was bliss for the two-child family who moved there from their cramped inner-city room. The furnishing of the flat was reconstructed to include many contemporary objects – such as a bed-sofa for father, the pullout-bed for the son, the dressing table with its puckered cloth for mother, the Stig Lindberg ashtray on the triangular table and father's small ashtray under the bed like a modern potty! Smoking was permissible anywhere, even in a bedroom with a baby.

Since the flat is a reconstruction, it has more furniture and textiles by famous, modern designers than real families of the time presumably could afford. One wanted to give a representative view of a 1950s flat.

The two-room flat in Hällefors is somewhat larger, and furnished as a result of a female study-project between ABF (the Workers' Educational Association) and the ordinary inhabitants of Hällefors. Firstly they studied the era, both socially and aesthetically, then they discussed furnishing. Finally they hunted objects and fitted out the flat as they imagined a two-child family with teenagers would have done at the end of the 1950s.

The living room is still the "best" room but the sofa is used as a bed at night, at any rate at the weekends. Father sleeps on the kitchen sofa during the week since he has to get up so early. His coffee thermos and lunchbox are placed out ready.

Above: The Stockholm suburb of Vällingby was inaugurated in 1954 as an example of the modern ABC town, the letters stand for Arbete (Work), Bostäder (Homes), Centrum (Centre). The architects Backström & Reinius designed the square and built the civic hall, Trappan, with a café and exhibition hall.

Right: A teenage girl's room as shown at Hällefors. The wallpaper is boldly patterned, like much else in the room. The dream was to have a bat armchair, a Nisse Strinning shelf and a transistor radio. Posters of Tommy Steele and Elvis Presley were everywhere; wide skirts and stiletto-heeled shoes were worn by every teenage girl.

Previous spread: The women's group at Hällefors has furnished a traditional living room with teak furniture, covered with green, grey and brown woollen fabrics. The TV is in its corner and a globe stands proudly on the sideboard. The textiles and deep-pile rug have modern patterns. The room is light and airy.

The TV is placed like an altar in its own corner of the living room, together with a raffia lamp, an African bust and patterned, artificial silk curtains. There is also a deep-pile rug and a table with black, tapering legs. The furnishing is both airy and functional but still has the mute quality of a traditional best room. Lena Larsson's ideas about the living room have not pervaded this one.

Left: Four people crowded into the bedroom. Mother and baby on the long wall, father in the pullout sofa with an ashtray on the floor under the bed, and a child in an extendable children's bed. A shiny quilt and lace-decorated sheets were standard.

Above, left: Contemporary details: a triangular teak table with Carl Arne Breger's TV-thermos, Stig Lindberg's chequered ashtray and coffee cup, Spisa ribb. And a deep-pile cushion in the armchair.

Above, right: Before TV, the radio gramophone was the holy piece of furniture. You could not only hear the whole world but also listen to 78-records and modern LPs and EPs. You could stack ten records at a time on the latest apparatus – true long-playing!

The Architect's Flat

One of the 1950s flats at Hällefors has been newly furnished by the adman and design collector Torbjörn Lenskog. It is a three-room flat – large and modernly conceived for its time. You had the chance to influence certain things, for example where a wall was placed. The contemporary furnishing is pure and austere. It includes a lot of furniture by famous designers, including Danish, Swedish and American. There is a strong influence from the H55 exhibition, which preferred a few designed objects to the usual abundance of mementoes and trinkets as "necessary feel-good features".

But there is also, of course, the obligatory string-shelf, in a larger version, with built-in cupboards with both glass doors and painted veneer sliding-doors in the typical dirty-yellow and grey-green 1950s colours. It takes up one long side of the living room. On the other, next to the lounge suite, there is a large, oblique-angled picture window – an innovation of that period. In one corner of the room, facing the dining room and behind the sofa, there is a reading space with a comfortable wicker chair by the Dane Hans Wegner.

Another innovation is the open room with integrated kitchen and dining room. The partition wall can be easily taken away. The kitchen is painted light yellow and has a grey linoleum floor, which meets the oak parquet of the dining room. There is a stainless steel sink and a fridge. There was, as yet, no freezer, but the kitchen still has a larder, with ventilation to the outside wall. The row of typical 1950s glass drawers for herbs and dry foodstuffs is mounted under the wall cupboard.

The dining room area has a dark-green contrast wall and modern Danish teak furniture designed by Hans Wegner in 1949. This furniture is still manufactured by Fritz Hansen. The three-legged chairs with the plywood seat and straight, tapering legs are stackable and were considered radical when they came.

The furniture architect Hans Wegner was knowledgeable in craftsmanship and came to be a master of chairs – he designed about 500 different ones – and a strong contributor to the Danish Modern movement, a concept that was just as famous as Swedish Modern in the 1950s.

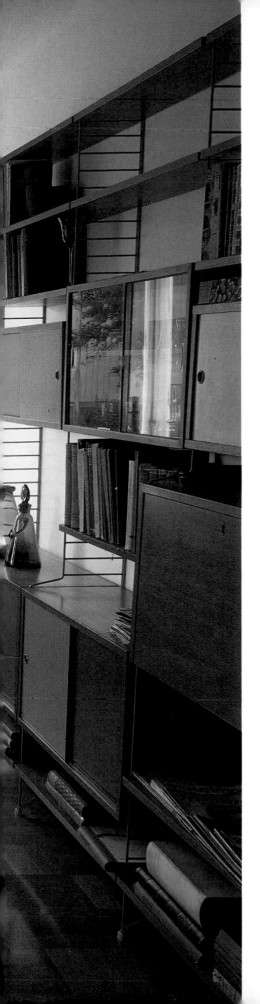

Previous spread, left: Hans Wegner is the favourite, with several chairs from his rich assortment. Here is an elegant wicker armchair with a teak frame, standing in the reading corner behind the sofa in the living room.

Previous spread, right: The living room could not have a more 1950s atmosphere! A dark-green contrast wall, teak furniture by Hans Wegner including the stackable, three-legged chairs, a salad bowl and tall teak candlesticks. The porcelain and chinaware are designed by Stig Lindberg.

Left: The white living room is lit from two directions – the balcony wall and the long wall with its angled picture window. The gently curved, brown sofa is Danish while the large kidney-shaped table is anonymous. The TV was designed Stig Lindberg for Luxor and a chair by the balcony window is a product by Charles Eames. Eric Höglund's rustic, coloured glassware stands here and there, like exclamation marks.

Below: We are used to seeing Arne Jacobsen's pedestal table and his chair Myran in more elegant surroundings, but we should not forget that they were designed as everyday furniture. In this 1950s kitchen they serve both for eating and other activities, such as sewing.

The 1960s

Pop, plastic, positivism and one million homes

Progress proceeds by leaps and bounds. It is doubtful if it ever went faster. Everything is positive. Lots of children are born. Jobs are concentrated to larger towns and people move from the countryside. Mostly to Stockholm and other major towns. But there aren't any flats! Not even the small one- and two-room flats from the 1920s, '30s and '40s are enough. People also want – and can afford – bigger homes. On top of all that, the old housing is beginning to go downhill, so that many flats are demolished.

The government therefore decides on the so-called "Million Programme": a million homes to be built in ten years (1965–1975).

The building industry lobbies for unit housing, that is to say pre-fabricated buildings assembled on site. Lennart Holm of the Building Research department designs a modular plan, 3M (the widths between the bearing girders), that the flat-units will be built according to. Six modules give twelve square metres. These are the measurements that govern most of the pre-fabricated houses: kitchens, rooms, halls, bathrooms. It is large-scale and extremely rationally conceived. Lennart Holm states quite seriously that "It must be better to build 1000 similar flats to a well thought-out plan than 50 according to 20 different plans".

The ground was levelled, all trees were taken away and a central crane on rails, which put all the housing elements in place, was erected. The buildings go up like houses of cards – walls with windows already in place, and bathrooms ready-fitted with toilets, that just need to be slotted in place.

Above: The super-modern on good terms with the traditional – the Italian Joe Colombo's black moulded-plastic chair, Elda, from 1965, back-to-back with Bruno Mathsson's chrome and leather revolving armchair, Jetson, designed in 1966 for Mathsson International.

Left: IKEA's furniture follows the trend. This is an interior with the company's own version of the revolving armchair, a laminated revolving table, a white, Greek deep-pile rug and yellow and orange decorations on the wall.

Below: The Dane Hans Wegner is the master of the well-made chair. He worked mostly in wood, but this armchair, the Bull Chair, from 1960, is from the range of tubular steel furniture he made in later years.

Previous spread: The housing shortage was to be eliminated in the 1960s; the goal was a million homes between 1965 and 1975. A colossal task which of course led to many mistakes and stereotype estates. But also to fresh ideas about space and function. This photo is from Storstugan in Täby and was shown at the City Museum's exhibition about the Million Programme in Stockholm during 2000.

But in their haste they forget the exterior: the environment and the infrastructure. People's well-being. Belief in standardisation and mass-production is so strong it is seen as life itself. They claim that it is no longer possible to return to small-scale construction and individually designed homes! They are stuck in the central crane.

In spite of this crassness, there are many good ideas behind the escalated speed of construction and the technology. The conflict arose from the demand to build quickly, to cut down on manpower and to use cheap, maintenance-free materials – which unfortunately proved to be "maintenance-impossible". Plastic paint that fell off, sheet metal façades that loosened, windows that rotted and plastic skirting-board and window frames that split. The buildings deteriorated and were worn out in no time. In spite of the large size of the flats, the well-planned bathrooms and kitchens with both fridge and freezer, two toilets, large balconies and much cupboard space, these homes became a kind of transit accommodation, while the occupiers were waiting for their own detached houses. There was, namely, quite a lot of small-scale housing in the Million Programme, even though we associate it today with the large, monolithic estates of Tensta, Rinkeby and Skärholmen in Stockholm and Rosengård in Malmö, amongst others.

Although the architects were forced to subordinate themselves to technology as never before, a number of exciting housing projects were built during the Million Programme era. Amongst these were Grindtorp in Täby, Ralph Erskine's house in Sandviken, the Film Institute at Gärdet in Stockholm and parts of Sergels Torg (the Haymarket skyscrapers in the middle of the 1950s and the Culture House by Peter Celsing at the end of the 1960s) in a kind of heavy, monumental and international concrete style.

The decade of consumption

Once people had their homes, they had to fill them. And this was done with the same speed and the same sort of cheap throwaway materials. Plastic spread out like a kind of universal carpet, useful for everything. Lamps, tables, chairs, household utensils, toys, carpets, just name it, were made in bright and gaudy colours, to be used as long as you felt like it and then thrown on the mountain of rubbish that was growing as high as the Himalayas.

Lena Larsson, the interior designer and lifestyle-debater, has often been unfairly accused of being the person who encouraged the Swedish people to buy, wear out, and throw away. Mostly throw away. But her idea was, rather, to get people to liberate themselves from "unnecessary duties, such as pleating pillow bands and polishing silver that you never used anyway". This would make time for socialising. People could live so that everybody, children and grownups alike, could move freely without having to worry about knocking down or breaking things. It was better to use cheap things or disposable articles and throw them away when they were worn out, to make time for other occupations, she reasoned.

Such ideas were born in an age of innocence, before a consciousness of environmental destruction and the earth's resources was even conceived. Everything was therefore eternal consumption. There was no end to anything. And rubbish, one did not even know what it was.

The growing number of designers loved plastic. It could be used for new forms and colours. It corresponded with Beatles songs, Carnaby Street and Mary Quant, the whole of Swinging London where everyone went for inspiration. That is, if they did not go all the way to the homeland of plastic, the USA, where Eero Saarinen and Charles Eames made chairs from moulded fibreglass as early as the 1950s, and Robin Day stackable plastic chairs in the 1960s. Chairs that came to flood the world in the same way as cheap, white plastic garden chairs do today.

German designer Dieter Rams used plastic in an unexpected aesthetic-functional way for the electronics company Braun, amongst others. He designed many household gadgets, transistors, clocks, shavers etc in the 1960s and '70s using a pure, Bauhaus style. The Italians also contributed to raising the status of plastic from cheap throwaway to high-class, with furniture and utensils. Joe Colombo went furthest with his total Furnishing Unit that consisted of a single form-moulded plastic unit for the bathroom, the kitchen or the whole house, that he squeezed into a cube. The Dane Verner Panton was also one of the plastic rascals. He hated white and designed rows of moulded plastic chairs with unconventional shapes and brilliant colours. Panton believed in the power of psychedelic colours and synthetic materials. He worked mostly in Switzerland where he felt more at home than in Denmark with its tradition of teak.

In Sweden, Hans Ehrich and Tom Ahlström designed plastic for practical household use. But Carl-Arne Breger was Sweden's real Mister Plastic, followed by Sigvard Bernadotte. They both designed everything from bowls and TV-thermoses to buckets and dustpans – all our everyday needs, in other words.

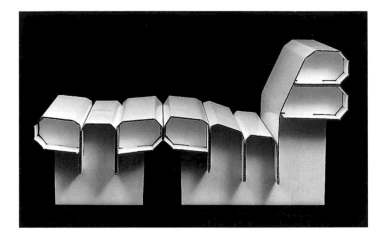

Above: Many conventional ideas were turned on their heads during the 1960s. Why not make furniture of cardboard? Like a kind of young and cheap disposable product. Jan Dranger and Johan Huldt, with their firm Innovator, exhibited this reclining armchair made of corrugated cardboard.

Left: These low, closely grouped houses with bright blue window frames inspired by the Mediterranean, were built at Kungshamra, Solna, during the late 1960s.

Below: The Englishman Ralph Erskine became established in Sweden and has become one of our most important architects. His own house in Drottningholm is built according to the principle of the double-arched roof. The façade is of raked cement. There is a similar office directly opposite.

The rise and fall of chipboard

The decade was characterised by the young, the happy and the easy. This is where the fantastic story of chipboard comes in. If I remember correctly, it was the furnishing magazine Allt i Hemmet that introduced chipboard as the cheap, do-it-yourself material for the home. Leif Qvist's creative drawings showed you how to saw, nail and screw and turn a piece of chipboard into a shelf or a bed. We dragged home seventeen kilos of chipboard board per person annually for several years. Guess if lots of sawing was done in cellars and hobby workshops! But everything did not quite match. For example, the last shelf in the bookcase was almost always half as wide as the others. One forgot that several millimetres disappeared at each sawing!

KF and IKEA latched on, selling chipboard furniture for millions and millions. KF called their chipboard furniture the Spika series, after a shelf that their textile manager Hedvig Block-Hedqvist found at Erik Karlström and incorporated in KF's range. You took the heavy boards home and put them together yourself. But at least they were correctly sawn!

I remember how we painted chipboards that sucked up litres of paint and how nylon tights snagged on the sharp, frayed corners. How flat and boring the beds with their unresilient polyether mattresses really were, and how wobbly the shelves, if they were not pushed into a corner. But it was new and fresh, and many people learned how to saw!

This chipboard furniture matched the flexibility of the age. It was supplemented by groovy, printed fabrics, low tables and sofas that you lay in rather than sat in – a kind of play and sprawl furniture. KF's Laban with its huge upholstery stuffed with polyether flock and covered with grass-green or orange corduroy could be found in most young homes together with Nisse shelving or IKEA's Ingo.

KF's Möbel-konsum (Furniture department) and IKEA opened their first stores about the same time in the middle of the 1960s. But it was not long before the founder of IKEA Ingvar Kamprad could, with his smart advertising and ever-increasing manufacture in Poland, undercut his competition and attract the customers. While Kamprad paid ten crowns for a chair made in Poland, it cost well over a hundred to make in Sweden!

Thanks to the young decorator Lennart Ekmark's progressive, radical and home-like interiors, the IKEA store at Kungens Kurva in Stockholm became an attractive and crowded goal for young families' excursions.

Above: Brightly coloured plastic took over our homes during the 1960s. Orange, above all, was popular, in everything from eggcups to TVs and radios. This photo is from the exhibition Seklets Spegel.

Left: Verner Panton adored colourful furniture. Here is a stool made from orange sheet metal, with Marco Zanuso's and Richard Sapper's folding radio on top.

Right: The 1960s were the chipboard decade. Homes began to be furnished for children, which continued during most of the 1970s. This bright chipboard-made home with simple, corduroy-covered furniture is from the KF catalogue. The favourite colours were brown and orange.

Thus, IKEA came to furnish the "People's Home" that legendary Social Democrat Per Albin Hansson had built up.

Now children were discovered and provided for. KF's Växa-med-Läxa furniture and the Kulan beds, which could be placed on top of each other, are classics of children's furniture. So too is Stephan Gip's chair, Robust, still one of the best children's chairs ever made.

Many of Form Design Centre's exhibitions and debates on lifestyles during the 1960s and 1970s revolved around children and the world of the young. The cheerful duo Annika Heijkenskjöld and Regina Ivarsson were in charge of this unique operation in Malmö. Erik Berglund founded the Furniture Institute in 1967, due to this increased consumption and the many families that wanted good, but cheap, furniture. The Institute's label, Möbelfakta, replaced the old VDN-mark as a sign of a tested and approved product. One of the most important areas for these tests was children's beds and furniture.

Above: Shelf-tables of chipboard, Kulan beds, foam rubber cushions and bright fabrics on the wall characterise children's rooms, that become more and more like wild adventure playgrounds. The needle felt carpet was everywhere, soft to play on, but a scourge for the allergic.

The Glass House at Kungsör

"I like the American feeling in this house", says advertiser and design collector Torbjörn Lenskog. "The flatness, and the light coming in from all sides".

Torbjörn, his wife, and a countless number of objects moved from Stockholm to a glass house in Kungsör in 1997. It was designed by Bruno Mathsson, situated on the main street and lit up like an exhibition hall. Which it had been. Bruno Mathsson, who had been inspired during a trip to the USA, designed twenty or so glass houses during the 1950s. This large one was built in 1954 for the furniture manufacturer Prenker in Kungsör and was used for exhibiting office furniture on the street side and as living quarters on the other. The house has had differing uses since then. At one stage it was a fast-food kiosk! Other Mathsson houses have met with similar fates, amongst them his own summer house Frösakull which has stood empty for a long time.

Bruno Mathsson was modern for his time. The shape of the house is inspired by the delta-shaped Draken fighter plane. It "hangs" from a double wall in the middle, with one wing somewhat cut off, which now accommodates the office and design collection. The whole house stands on a cast concrete, heated floor. The floor was laid with slate and mosaic – something that Torbjörn Lenskog is trying to re-create, piece by piece. Soon the parquet of the living room will be changed back to small, light-grey pieces of mosaic! Mathsson's windows were very modern for their time: triple-glazing which still works perfectly. Doors lead from several rooms to the paved backyard, where arduous cultivation has had to give way to potted plants, some chairs and a table for meals.

From the small hall at the main entrance, you enter a large open hall-room that is also used as a dining room. The walls are covered with well-filled bookshelves, here as in most other rooms. The light comes in from above and bounces attractively on the black slate

Left: Looking from the living room with its open fireplace into the dining room – an extension of the hall which runs like an axle through the house. It has slate flooring, overhead light and walls with bookshelves. The dining table and chairs are by Hans Wegner and the ceiling lamp is by Gino Sarfatti.

Above: The large living room is suffused by light from every direction. Classic furniture from Ray and Charles Eames, Arne Jacobsen, Axel Larsson stands in groups – all from Torbjörn Lenskog's vast collection. The parquet flooring will be replaced by mosaic, as designed by Bruno Mathsson in the 1950s.

Previous spread: The private side of the house faces onto a narrow stone-paved terrace. Large windows alternate with doors and black wooden wall surfaces. The overhang is a metre wide and rainwater runs straight down into a narrow gravel bed below. It is all somewhat reminiscent of a Japanese garden.

floor. Then the dining room/hall narrows again to transform into a corridor with bathroom and bedrooms along the sides towards the "nose of the Draken plane".

The irregular shaped living room with glass walls from ceiling to floor, an open fireplace and a gently sloping, panelled pentroof, is on the other "wing". Bruno Mathsson's wish for windows from ceiling to floor led him to experiment with floor-heating as early as the 1950s.

The main room is filled with furniture that are all design classics. Mostly from the 1960s, but also an early Josef Frank table and Ray and Charles Eames's luxurious leather armchair with footstool, No. 670, from 1956. Arne Jacobsen's black leather armchair, Ägget, designed for the SAS hotel in Copenhagen, is another classic. So too are a couple of Axel Larsson armchairs with plaited leather strips. The Danish Eilersen sofa is more recent.

It is difficult to say whether this living room is part of the Lenskog family's home or part of their collection. Torbjörn's interests are so closely woven that there is no real boundary between work and everyday life. For this almost incredible collecting has become work, leading to both the exhibition Returnity at the National Museum, 1996–1997, and his "own" museum for industrial design at Bångbro in Bergslagen, which opened in the spring of 1999, and has now moved to Hällefors.

Torbjörn Lenskog was originally one of our most successful admen, and founded and built up the Arbman & Lenskog agency. After a score of 20th "gold eggs" and a "platinum egg", the finest award in advertising, he felt it was enough. Now he wanted to dedicate himself to his hobby and passion: 20th century design. The money earned from advertising financed a collection which includes everything from the world's most famous designers – chairs, tables, shelves, lighting, chinaware, radio sets, household gadgets, and a whole Aalto room – to masses of more or less anonymous everyday objects, from plastic boxes and thermos flasks to whisks and hair-pins. No wonder it takes a huge house and a couple of permanent exhibition halls to hold it all!

Above: The kitchen is both modernised and restored. The original, light-grey mosaic floor is an example of this. A wide door leads out to the terrace. The pedestal table is designed by Eero Saarinen from Finland, and the chairs by the Dane, Hans Wegner.

Right: The house, designed by Bruno Mathsson in 1954, is divided into an exhibition part and a private area. A wall made of local stone divides public and private. A wrought-iron fence and a black door mark out a definite boundary between the parts. A corrugated plastic roof covers the terrace along the whole width of the house.

The 1970s

The decade of children and communes

The position that children had begun to assume at the end of the 1960s was strengthened during the 1970s, which turned into a real "children's decade". The large 1940s generation had grown up and had children of their own. It was a radical era with village communities, political manifestations, repercussions of the 1968 student revolt, feminism, group therapy... Accounts were settled with the parent generation, which also included their way of living, bringing up children – and furnishing. Away with the obligation to lay the table with a white cloth, to eat with several sets of cutlery and of forcing children to sit quietly!

Old and young ate together in large sittings, with the pot directly on the table. The damask-woven linen cloths were dyed mauve and were used for home-sewn hippie clothes. It was a practical decade above all, and for the first time people also wanted to be careful with the environment. The oil crisis of 1973 contributed to a natural restraint in what had previously been uninhibited consumption. The spirit of the commune included a simple life and "doing it yourself". So people sawed and fixed things up. Repainted and wallpapered. Children were a part of everything, too.

Magazines were full of advice and tips for the handyman. And the paint manufacturers shouted, "paint on Saturday, party on Sunday", referring to the new thixotropic paints that covered with just one coat. Things were painted brightly and often. If it wasn't painted it was decorated with textiles: on furniture, as table cloths, curtains, drapes or just hung up on the wall.

The newly-started 10-Group designed exciting patterns that were printed by Borås Wäfveri. Vivianne Sjölin was employed by IKEA's textile department. Thanks to her nose for good textiles, IKEA's

fabrics became a spearhead and an area where IKEA did not copy but was, rather, copied. Some of their showpieces were Inez Svensson's simple cross-striped fabrics Strix and Strax, that were sold by the thousands of metres, and Sven Fristedt's colourful organically patterned fabrics.

The 1970s was, in fact, an over-patterned decade. It became a real mess of patterns when everything crowded in the same room. For there were patterns on everything from household paper, splash guards, plastic mugs, hotplate covers and saucepans, to sofa fabrics, wallpaper, curtains, cloths, duvet covers, towels, plastic mats. You could not find plain-coloured duvet covers or even white towels. Borås Wäfveri turned out a hundred new patterns each season. Only a few of these were "designed" and thought out as part of a colour collection. The boldly patterned, non-iron, resin-treated duvet covers were the worst, assaulting us with their scratchy surfaces and gaudy colours. God help you if you woke up between them on a pallid winter's day.

From nursery to adventure playground

Life revolved a great deal around children. The living room was turned into a children's playroom. If this was not possible, the children's bedrooms were turned into adventure playgrounds with wall bars, gymnastic rings, dens and swings. The bed was often put on extended legs or on top of several boxes with space for a den underneath.

It was a robust, "correct", velour era with a lot of freedom but also a great many constraints. Pity those who did not fit in or who rebelled against the radical codex that the old student union occupiers had laid down!

But the "revolutionary chants" resulted, amongst other things, in KF's (the Cooperative Society) large investment in both basic clothes and basic furniture – the first later scoffed at (because of their synthetic materials), the latter still partly in production. We got a basic sofa that was wide enough to serve as an extra bed, beautiful armchairs by Kersti Sandin and Lars Bülow and retro Windsor-style chairs and dining tables.

This was 1978. IKEA had strengthened its position much earlier as furniture store Number One for "young families with more imagination than money". There were long, winding queues every Saturday to the child-friendly stores with their plastic-ball play areas and meatballs at family prices. Sofas, beds and tables were carried home in flat cardboard boxes with their accompanying Allen

Above: KF's catalogues had a matter-of-fact tone, focusing on a child-friendly, durable home. The sofa San Marino had polyether upholstery covered with green stretch towelling. This sofa, a table on wheels, Combinett shelving and curtain fabric Lövet, by Susanne Grundell, were on the 1973/74 catalogue cover.

Left: As a reaction to foreign, mushy fabric patterns, ten textile designers started the 10-Group in 1970, opening a shop in Stockholm. This poster shows their first patterns.

Previous spread: People did not care much about historic values in the 1970s. Things were there to be used and have fun with. This piano, for example, became much more lively in orange with white daisies.

keys, and then put together with much wailing and gnashing of teeth. If you included your own work, maybe they were not quite as cheap as you thought.

The home was furnished with soft, low, sit-and-lie furniture where the children could romp around. There was not any real space for granny and granddad.

Neofunctionalism on good terms with Swedish wood

Jan Dranger and Johan Huldt, with their company Innovator, led the young furniture league during the whole 1970s. Their knock-down chair Stuns was sold to KF, and a similar one to IKEA. The Tech Trolley was made of black-lacquered metal plate and heralded the high tech era. Most things were sold through their own shops, Basic Design, but the big deal came with the contract they signed with Englishman Terence Conran and his Habitat chain. This laid the ground for international co-operation that soon resulted in 90 percent of their turnover going for export.

Lindau & Lindekrantz also manufactured tubular steel furniture

Above and below: Carl Johan De Geer and Sven Fristedt were two bright stars on the textile designers' firmament. They both made powerful patterns in unusual colour combinations, both wild in their different ways. Below, a bedroom with Carl Johan De Geer's swirling, red-and-white fishes on the wall. The other bedroom has a wall covered with a black-and-white Sven Fristedt fabric, Pärona. A variation of the Pärona fabric is used as a bedcover.

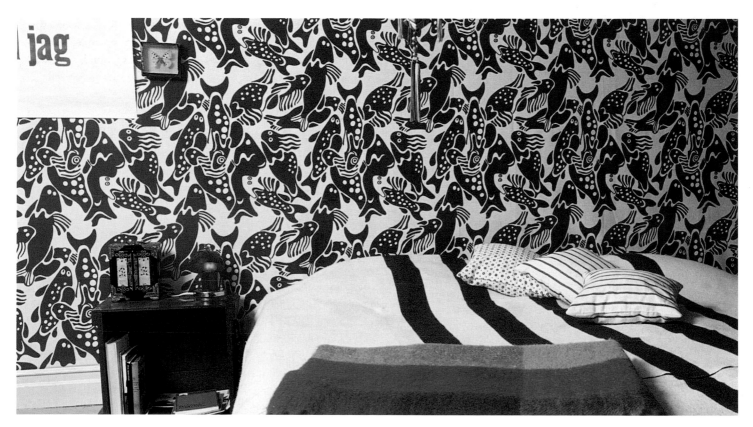

with corduroy coverings, but aimed at a more discriminating set of customers than the young radicals at Innovator. Börge Lindau and Bo Lindekrantz combined a new Bauhaus spirit with a modern 1970s style in colourful furniture; amongst these, bar stools for the kitchen, canvas and tubular steel directors' chairs, and polyester moulded sofas.

Of course wooden furniture was still made, since not everyone was young and wanted to live on the floor. Åke Axelsson, the master of chairs, began teaching at Konstfack (Stockholm's University College of Arts, Crafts and Design) and disseminated his profound knowledge of wood to his pupils. He studied the harmony of antique constructions – Clismo chairs and simple laced chairs – and made new chairs in the same spirit for the House of Parliament, the College of Economics and for the Culture House in Leksand.

Norells, Hans Ehrlin and Karl Andersson & Söner also provided us with classical furniture, as did Bruno Mathsson, but he had now abandoned bentwood in preference for slender, stainless steel constructions. The super-ellipse table with buckle-legs, made in collaboration with his friend and colleague Piet Hein, was one example, the armchairs Karin and Jetson are others – the latter being an elegant Swedish version similar to Charles Eames' black leather armchair, Model no 670. He received inverted praise for his armchair Jetson: at last he has broken free from the tyranny of fixed sitting angles!

Above: One of the first pieces of high-tech furniture in Sweden was the Tech Trolley, made by Jan Dranger and Johan Huldt of Innovator. A bestseller.

Far right: Innovator's international breakthrough came in 1972 with the simple and inexpensive armchairs Stuns and M1. They were sold by both IKEA and KF. The marketing was new and bold.

Left: There really was no end of colour. Here the whole kitchen has been covered in brown and pink, even the gasstove! It will last as long as it lasts, one reasoned.

Right: IKEA's catalogue from 1973 espoused simple, young living. This cover shows the bed-sofa Tajt, covered in blue denim. The yellow carpet and striped wallpaper serve to emphasize the Swedishness. Ingvar Kamprad's company was still small and manageable. He had only just started to pry into the international market.

A Young and Cheap
Way of Living

A young family with a mother who studied and a father who had just started work did not have a lot of money, even though times were good. This couple chose a three-room flat in the Stockholm suburb of Husby, while waiting for their dream house. The building-society flat from HSB (The Tenants' Association Building Society) was flexible in so far as one could choose different "colour packages" for wall-paper, kitchen cupboards and bathrooms. There was also the possi-bility of moving walls and making small changes oneself.

Inga and Sven furnished their 76 square metre "yellow package" flat with cheap, light, furniture and a mixture of old and new. There was no point in investing in expensive furnishings since the years with small children would mean a great deal of wear and tear. It was better to wear it out first and only later buy things one wanted to live with for a long time. This was the sensible 1970s way of reasoning.

So the living-room floor was covered in grey linoleum, with a round sea-grass mat and five light wicker armchairs, instead of a wool carpet and sofa. The ubiquitous Spika shelves are even found in this home, painted cornflower blue and laid horizontally as a long bench under the window, instead of standing up. The same blue colour was used throughout the whole flat – in many small details, often to match the yellow, another popular colour that was bought in vast amounts. The cushions in the armchairs, alternately blue or patterned and with a zip at the back, were sewn by Inga herself.

The other half of the living room was left free for playing. An old bookcase and two so-called Carl Westman chairs from the turn of the 20th century were also painted blue. A folded gate-legged table stood next to the wall and a blue cotton rag mat covered the floor; nice for playing on.

Blue and yellow was accentuated even more in the kitchen and dining room. Some of the cupboard doors were taken down and the cupboards were painted blue inside. The blue oilcloth was comple-mented by the sun-yellow curtains and the yellow plastic utensils – which presumably contained cadmium! But this was unheard of at the time. Even this room was made fun for the children. Sven made

a blackboard, using special paint, along the wall of the dining room and above this he put up cork tiles, as a practical notice board for messages etc.

The children's bedroom was furnished for more play and activities. Their daughter Katarina's bed stood on red Tore boxes from IKEA, with a curtained den underneath. There was a small slide from the end of the bed and plush-covered cushions, red plastic crates for building with, jumping on or storing things in. The wall was papered with a colourful flower and wild strawberry pattern.

When all these bright colours were installed, Inga and Sven had almost managed to conjure away the bureaucrat-beige living-room wallpaper and the dining room's unimaginative flower-mush wallpaper. All this within the framework of what was allowed, for there were strict rules for what you could or could not do!

Left: The yellow doors came with the kitchen, but they were livened up with large, intensive blue knobs. The cupboard walls, where the doors have been taken away, are painted the same blue as the linoleum on the floor. There is a strip of plastic printed with blue ducks over the sink. Cut to the right size and put up with double-sided tape. Easy to take away and change when you feel like it!

Right: The dining room is really blue and yellow. In spite of the wimpish flower-patterned wallpaper, the overall impression is lively, thanks to the sun-yellow cotton curtains, the blue oilcloth and yellow plastic utensils. The chairs are Norwegian, Trip Trap, and adjustable from baby to adult. One wall has a blackboard at the bottom and a cork noticeboard at the top.

Previous spread: Inga and Sven reasoned that it would be better to have cheap and simple things when the children were small, and buy more expensive things later. So they bought five wicker chairs and a round, plastic laminated table. A blue painted Spika shelf serves as a long bench under the window. Cane venetian blinds hang in the window instead of curtains. A yellow metal lamp from IKEA hovers overhead.

With Lake Mälaren Outside the Window

When, in 1975, architect Bengt Hidemark and his wife Vera saw the Functionalist apartment block at Norr Mälarstrand in Stockholm they knew that this was where they wanted to live. Even before they saw the flat itself, Bengt Hidemark had sketched out the probable position and function of the different rooms on a paper napkin. Nine months later, when the flat had been bought, his guesses proved to be true.

The flat, which is very light and beautiful, is almost on the top floor of a building designed by Björn Hedvall in 1930. The windows are unusually large and well-proportioned. The large French windows facing the waters of Riddarfjärden open onto a terrace-like balcony that links outside with inside. Even during the winter you can sit in this part of the living room and drink your coffee in indoor warmth although the doors are wide open.

The flat has the classic 1930s open room formation, with a well thought-out axiality. From the hall you see straight through the dining room – originally planned as a library with an open fireplace – towards the living room and the balcony with its magnificent view. The flat is also open on the east-west axis, from the music room, to the long living room and to the workroom with its windows facing south and west.

The wide doorways to the music room and the workroom have sliding doors with panes of hand-blown glass. A rarity from that era.

Bengt and Vera Hidemark have been careful with the genuine details of the flat for two reasons: they are beautiful and they are historic. In their characteristic way they also tell us something about the middle class lifestyle in the 1930s, for example the numerical bell system in the serving passage, to ring for the maid. Or the staff lift outside the kitchen door.

Above: Bengt and Vera Hidemark are aesthetes with a feel for beautiful eye-catchers. Different Japanese objects share Josef Frank's glass trolley with its red-lacquered handle, designed at the beginning of the 1940s.

Right: The large flat on Norr Mälarstrand is beautifully lit, having windows in three directions. Looking from the workroom through the living room, with its plants next to the balcony, and on to the suite by the French window that opens eastward towards the City Hall. The furniture is a mixture of Alvar Aalto, inherited antiques and Bruno Mathsson.

Previous spread: The open part of the living room, with the terrace-like balcony facing the water of Riddarfjärden, is like an indoor veranda. Sitting in the sofa, which is a wedding present from Copenhagen, you can drink coffee even if there is snow outside. The sun warms up the room and the plants flourish.

Left: There is a magnificent view from the worktable. Bookshelves cover both walls and everywhere lies books, sketches and other sources of inspiration lie around. The table in the middle of the room is one of the extensions of the dining table.

Above: The music room has a trim, English "apartment-adapted" grand piano. From here you can see the living room suite with its round table and Karin chairs by Bruno Mathsson, as well as a 1970s lamp, Bumling, from the Lyktan studio. Notice the glazed sliding door between the rooms.

The kitchen has been left in its original guise, without a lot of modern wall-cupboards. Nor has the door to the maid's bedroom been removed, which is usual in most older flats of this type. Bengt Hidemark has, on the other hand, glazed the doors of the wall cupboard in the serving galley to create a more airy feeling.

There is not as much trace of the 1970s era, when they moved in, as there is of the light, airy and classical Functional style represented here by both Bruno Mathsson and Alvar Aalto, whose furniture dominates in a successful symbiosis with inherited antiques.

"We were striving for a light and harmonic timelessness," relates Bengt Hidemark, who has himself designed buildings rooted in the classical style.

All the walls and ceilings have been painted white, the floors are laid with beautiful oak parquet and have light carpets. Even the

Above: There are two practical folding shelves left from the 1930s in the serving passage, opposite the china cupboard. Above this is the numbered bell system that shows from which room the maid is being called.

Right: Three large windows light up the dining room, which also features an open fireplace. The oval table of masur birch is designed by Bengt Hidemark, the chairs by Jack Ränge, a version of Gemla's classic.

furniture is of pale wood with natural white coverings.

The oval dining table of masur birch is unique, designed by Bengt Hidemark himself. It has two extensions that can also function as separate tables. Together they are 4.40 metres long and can easily seat 25 guests.

The airy workroom with its large windows facing the water is where Bengt has his creatively overloaded worktable on which sketches, paper, new and old books about architecture and design are piled up. The walls are covered with bookshelves, and where there are not books there is art. Vera, who has been a teacher for many years, also has her worktable in this room.

Artists' Homes

Where imagination and enthusiasm prevail

Some homes you enter just smell of personality. Where furniture, colours and objects form new symbioses and where you cannot say that this is Fifties, Functionalist or whatever. There is just this unique and personal mix that belongs to the inhabitant of that home.

Artistic people often live in such houses. People who are either working artists or are borne up by a creative passion for the home, renovation and artefacts. Meagre economic resources also contribute to personal solutions and imaginative re-use, irrespective of whether it's a case of waking a whole barn from its slumber, or of furnishing a minimal space for use as an eating area for many.

The Old Barn

When Gösta and Viveka Wallmark sailed to Bläse on north Gotland in 1986, the old limestone barn of 480 square metres stood empty and ramshackle. It was built in the middle of the 19th century as a stable, shed and workshop for the chalk works. When the works closed in 1954 there was no further need for such a huge building. It was used for a while as a broiler farm where some of the workers got a job. But even this came to an end, and the barn stood there as an empty counterpart to the chalk works.

For an artist who needed space, Gösta Wallmark reasoned, it would not be such a bad idea to have a barn of that size. Buying it was cheap, but not the restoration. The inside walls were built up with cinder blocks, the floor was laid with wide pine planks and insulated, electricity and water were installed. The living room was given a beautiful white tiled oven, a so-called Wasa stove, which heats up the whole part of the house that is lived in, about half the total area.

There is an unusual feeling of harmony in the house that, according to Gösta Wallmark, can be due to the placing of the walls and their deep window niches. Instead of one straight central wall running through the house, the long walls are somewhat displaced in relation to each other. The windows and glass doors are also somewhat displaced which gives an almost, but not quite, symmetrical impression; in the same way that a row of Greek temple columns have different distances between them to trick the eye. Even the window arches differ. The bricklayer had his own opinions on how the windows should be built, Gösta had others. But the result was a similar harmony, building on small dissonances.

Openness is important. From the large hall with its clinker floor, worthy of a French palace, you step through glazed double doors into the heart of the house – the large room with a kitchen on one of its short walls, the workbench as a kind of divider, and a huge

dining table in the middle of the floor, balanced by a dark sideboard on the other short wall facing the studio. A row of windows and a French window beside the kitchen let in an abundance of southerly light.

The room turns northwards, and here the floor is a step higher. It is darker in this area, both because the walls have been left a natural grey – the others are whitewashed – and because only one small window lets light seep in. The Wasa stove stands here, bookshelves cover the walls and two sofas form a pleasant sitting area. An evening or winter place, if you like.

All the furnishing is aesthetic and austere, there is neither more nor less than necessary.

"Sometimes it's good not to have so much money", explains Viveka Wallmark, "Then you are forced to wait for the right moment and don't make hasty purchases."

She is thinking of the time at an auction when she told Gösta: "Bid 200!" So he made the bid and then wondered: "What did we buy?"

Yes, they had bought a pile of solid birch planks that were enough for both the dining table in the middle of the large room, for the workbench in the kitchen and for a very long, useful table out on the terrace.

A lot of things in this house have been built up in the same painstaking way. They found something that would be suitable; a church pew, a discarded Bertoia armchair or a pile of planks. In the

Left: The walls in the large room are white, the planks on the floor are treated with soap and the ceiling glazed white. The furniture is consciously austere – a home-made, light grey table with looped chairs stands in the middle of the floor on a large kelim carpet. A smaller breakfast table with two basketwork chairs stand next to one of the windows, where you can catch the morning light. Gösta Wallmark has built the kitchen workbench from birch planks and Gotland limestone with shelves for cookery books, bottles of wine and so forth on the outside, and kitchen cupboards on the inside. Behind the open shelving, the wall has been tiled white. Here the floor is painted light grey, ending in an semicircle towards the double garden door – not only a way of marking out the kitchen area, but also more practical than the soap-treated planks in the rest of the room. The painting is by Gösta Wallmark.

Previous spread: The long limestone barn from the mid-19th century has been turned into a magnificent home with studios. Two French windows open towards the south on the long side.

hands of two practical people the result has been beautiful sitting areas, functional tables and neat transitions from inside to outside. An example of the latter is a grey-painted kitchen floor that connects in a curve to the glazed double doors out to the garden.

The studio ceiling is twice as high (page 140). There is a balcony over some parts of the living room and with an opening down towards the studio. Everything is borne up by four steel columns and large windows have been let into the north east wall. Outside the studio there is a favourite spot, the enclosed terrace – actually the frame of yet another old barn, with the roof pulled down but the walls and the cement floor left. Here you can imagine that you're in Provence, because it is windless between the walls and warm enough for grapes, magnolia and other Mediterranean plants. A long church pew and the home-made table, both painted light grey, under a rust-coloured parasol makes this an ideal place for long, agreeable meals. Especially since Gösta likes to let Maria Callas play from his studio with its fine acoustics.

The garden on the south side of the house is open and park-like, shaded by a huge tree. There are a couple of sitting areas that catch the sunset and a kitchen garden furthest away. The beautiful light grey, wooden stairs from the kitchen link the inside with the outside in a natural and convenient way. Viveka has her pottery workshop on this side, also with French windows, that open on to a foundation stone with steps down to the grass. Of all the French windows Gösta has designed, he is most pleased with these, due to their successful proportions.

Above: The deep window niches have different shaped arches. Most of the walls are whitewashed.

Right: A step leads to the cosy, so-called evening area of the large room. It features a tiled oven, TV, bookshelves and comfortable seats. Two furniture classics – a Bertoia chair and a Bruno Mathsson armchair each have their own corners.

Left: There is a wall-enclosed area outside the studio where you can sit and eat, from early spring to late autumn. A church pew and a long home-made table provide room for many guests. This area used to be yet another barn, of which the cement floor and part of the walls are left, contributing to the character of a real room, but without a roof. It is warm and windless here.

Above: The thin-barred French windows lead in to Viveka Wallmark's pottery workshop. You come out to the garden via a foundation stone down narrow wooden steps to a welcoming sitting-area in which to take a break, or maybe coffee.

From Small Studio to a Home

Ten years ago, Krister Wallfält acquired a studio consisting of a room with "cooking possibilities" in an old house near Nytorget in Stockholm. Altogether it was 47 square metres. The "kitchen" consisted of a double hotplate on a chipboard shelf and the toilet was tiny, smelling of mould. The studio was not much to speak of either – a scarcely six-foot high attic space.

When his family increased to include a partner with teenage daughter, he found another place for his studio and rebuilt the 47 square metres into a home for three. This meant shoehorning in all the different functions. Luckily Krister was not only a qualified cabinet maker from Carl Malmsten's school, but also an experienced sailor and boat builder. Thus he knew all about getting maximum efficiency from minimal space. And he could do all the carpentry himself.

The toilet was replaced, the walls were tiled. An old zinc bathtub is an additional extra, which leans against the wall when not in use. He devoted a lot of care to the kitchen for two reasons. Partly because the family was very fond of food and partly because his partner Lena Sundkvist had worked at upmarket restaurants Greitz and Grythyttan. Making food for a whole company is an everyday thing, even in the minimal kitchen that Krister conjured up in the corridor between the daughter's room and the small dining room by the staircase. A four square metre passage with three doors and a window is now pressed into use for great culinary achievements. The stove is built into the widened window niche surrounded by robust, oiled working surfaces that Krister has created from old planks taken out from various places in the house. Shelves for kitchen utensils have been slipped in under the ceiling and a really cool pantry installed around the pipes of the outer wall. Lena can fold out a round-cornered tabletop when she needs a work surface.

It may look impossible, but eight people can just about fit into

the minimal dining room, which is strongly reminiscent of a ship's galley. But in compensation the house has a large, leafy inner-city garden. Summer parties are held here and in order to make the carrying of food and crockery easier, Krister has installed a "goods lift" from the window!

The large room is in the attic itself. Today it looks larger and more airy because Krister was allowed to remove the floor of the upper loft. In this way, he gained almost a metre. Even one of the long walls under the sloping roof has been taken out, creating room for books, a music system and a filing cabinet for designs and sketches. Light comes in from three overhead windows. Everything is painted white up here, of course, to emphasize the feeling of space. The floor is treated with white-pigmented oil.

As long as Lena's daughter lives at home, in the room next to the kitchen, all Krister and Lena's activities must co-exist in the attic – music, work, socialising and sleeping. With the sailor's feeling for making use of impossible spaces, Krister has managed to find room for a double bed in one corner, behind a bookshelf which divides off the music and living room area. Next to the staircase he has even built an open fireplace, narrow and angled out towards the room to give as wide a hearth as possible. Shelves and cupboards have been cleverly built in here and there, for example the glass cupboard for ornamental objects behind the chess table – an empty space that Krister found between the inner and outer walls.

Despite its minimal space, Krister and Lena's house is an exceedingly well-filled home, not least concerning the art, sculptures and odd mementoes that they both love to arrange in attractive ways.

Left: The attic room contains a surprising amount. It looks much larger thanks to white-painted walls, ceiling, beams and three skylights. Next to the stairs there is a sitting area with chess table, comfortable chairs and an open fireplace, made by Krister. The glass cupboard is built into the wall.

Above: The large leafy garden in the middle of Stockholm, near Nytorget, features a greenhouse and several different sitting areas. This is where Krister Wallfält and Lena Sundkvist gather friends for big parties. A sail can be stretched up if rain threatens.

Previous spread, left: The staircase is a heavenly blue dream. Krister has removed the old paint and repainted it with blue and white egg-oil paint. The staircase is full of paintings, his own, Lena's and other artists', together with model boat and sculptured objects.

Previous spread, right: There are deep shelves for books, music, storage of sketches etc, along one wall of the living room. The bed is placed nearest the window, partly hidden by a transverse bookshelf with TV.

Above: In the dining room, which is barely larger than the kitchen, is a built-in bench, shelves for bowls and glasses and folding tabletops – all in best naval fashion. All the carpentry has been done using old planks taken from the house.

Right: The heart of the house – the kitchen – is only 4 square metres but contains everything that Lena Sundkvist, who is a professional, needs to make a feast for a whole company. Thanks to her partner Krister Wallfält's boat building and sailing knowledge, they get maximal use of minimal space.

The House on the Island

When artists AnnMari Brenckert-Tjerned and Leif Tjerned found the white archipelago house on the island of Kungshatt in Lake Mälaren, it had stood empty for so long that branches had grown in through the roof. The previous owner had a peculiar relationship with his house – on the one hand it was primitive, with an outdoor privy, water from a well, a bowl for washing up in the hall, decaying floors and single paned windows without putty. On the other hand it had Spanish arches, colossal four-poster beds with upholstered bed-heads, wall-to-wall carpets and various 1970s fripperies.

"We came in November," relates AnnMari, "It was freezing. And there was no jetty so the first thing we did was to build one with the roof of one of the four-poster beds. They were solid oak planks from the island, so they still hold."

AnnMari and Leif Tjerned's philosophy is simple and clear: we need space to paint and sculpt. We need peace and quiet. As for most artists, money is in short supply, therefore we have to live cheaply. Being able to fish and grow things ourselves we can combine our own upkeep with natural and wholesome food.

In the crevices between the rocks on this hilly island there are potatoes, beans, cabbages, broccoli and more, enough to last at least until Christmas. Lake Mälaren provides fish – what else is needed?

Houses were built early on Kungshatt, thanks to several brick works on the island. It has been discovered that the cellar of the house dates from the 17th century. The rest has been subsequently built on or rebuilt such as the glass veranda, for example, which is typical for the turn of the last century. The present kitchen is from the 1940s with a stove in one corner, but the sink is new, installed by Leif and AnnMari last year when they sank a new well. There is a bathroom but still only an outside privy.

"We wrap up well when we go there in the winter!" says AnnMari.

Some of the living room furniture is from the 1940s. This is

partly due to lack of money but also because they are well made, including a heavy three-piece suite covered in dark blue plush. The kitschy 1970s furniture from the upper floor will be removed gradually, mainly because it is very much the worse for wear.

Going through the rooms on the top floor is a journey through cultural clashes. From the dark, overloaded 1970s room you come into a lighter room filled with AnnMari's inherited white and gold Empire furniture. From there you emerge onto the veranda with deep-red Windsor-style chairs from the 1940s. You are exposed to the next clash in the room beside the Empire room. The unmoveable

Left: Time has stood still in the glass veranda outside the living room. There is an almost Chekovian feel to the flaking, once-white walls, the benches, the barred windows and the old armchair from which you can watch the sunset.

Above: Water has just been installed in the kitchen. Previously the washing-up was done in the small hall next to the kitchen. The kitchen walls are painted in a beautiful blue. Everywhere there are signs of cultivation in the form of glass jars with conserved vegetables.

Previous spread: The old summer house on the island of Kungshatt has lived many lives, both before and after its heyday at the start of the 20th century. Today it is inhabited by two artists, who are renovating it carefully, growing ecological food and fishing in the lake.

Left: Looking out from the living room to the large veranda with its long row of windows facing the garden greenery and Lake Mälaren. A fragile curtain lets through the light and filters it poetically – a perfect transition from inside to outside.

Above: The living room in this old house on the island was last rebuilt in the 1970s, when the arch and the columns came about. The large panorama window facing the water was also installed then. The solid plush furniture and the pedestal table are from the 1940s.

double bed has a red, upholstered, buttoned, imitation leather bed-head with two small angels. A memento from the previous owner. The wallpaper is from the 1940s and the gold-framed painting is inherited.

In a way, AnnMari and Leif Tjerned's home gives us an important eye-opener about home aesthetics. Does everything have to be so thorough? So trendy, stylistically correct and uniform? Maybe you feel best if you don't have to care so much. Let it be an adventure to move from room to room, from memory to memory, with all the layers visible.

Above: The sturdy bed with the strange bed head made of red, upholstered, imitation leather, is built-in and cannot be moved. The 1940s wallpaper, gold-framed painting, and the African khanga cloth on the bed gives the room a "cultural breadth".

Right: The veranda on the upper floor is just made for quiet breakfasts. Creepers climb up the well-crafted woodwork and you can see the white boats in the distance on their way to Drottningholm.

The 1980s

Unique furniture for a wealthy generation

Extremes are nearly always followed by other extremes. Thus the collective, child-friendly, do-it-yourself 1970s were followed by an individualistic decade that put unique design, larger apartments and an obsession with money first. Maybe it was a weariness of the practical and the tried and tested that made way for both Post-modernism and artistic individuality. Furniture purchased more for the designer's name, during the 1980s, than for its function. Post-modernism was born in Italy where the Memphis group, led by architect Ettore Sottsass, started a small revolution with bizarre furniture that irreverently borrowed and mixed elements from past centuries. We were both delighted and shocked by the fashion for sloping tables, spillikin-shelves and chairs shaped like antique columns.

The desire – and maybe the need – to break with the weighing and measuring of the Furniture Institute also showed itself in Sweden. Here in the form of the exhibition Provokationer (Provocations) at the Culture House in 1982, where much of the furniture was rather humorous objects than functional articles.

A response came immediately from the professor of architecture Sven Thiberg, former president of Svensk Form (Swedish Design), who said: "Post-modernism is vulgar showing off, a mishmash of historical fragments. It concerns itself only with the surface and ignores the substance."

Above: Jonas Bohlin's 1981 exam-
ination chair, Concrete, created a great
fuss. Was this a chair or a work of art?
It stands as a rusty work of art outside
Källemo Möbler in Värnamo. Here in its
original shape – concrete and iron.

Left: Two experimental chairs: Jasper
Morrison's super-light, minimalist glue-
laminated wood chair from 1988 and
Philppe Stark's three-legged leather
armchair, J.Lang from 1984.

Previous spread: John Kandell's shelf,
Pilaster, has become an icon in most
design-conscious homes. It comes in
birch and cherry, white glazed, black or
red. The chair, Fax, is also by John
Kandell.

Looking back, one can now see that it was, in fact, time to move on. Much in the way of good design and durable function had already been attained. It was time for originality. One interior designer who gave utilitarian furniture a "post-modern" playfulness was Olle Anderson. His lamps and brightly painted cupboards found their way into many homes. John Kandell, Mikael Löfström and Jonas Bohlin also turned things on their head, making furniture in surprising colours and materials.

When Jonas Bohlin exhibited his chair, Concrete, at the Konstfack student exhibition in 1981, many people even spoke of a paradigmatic shift. A new way of life, a new way of thinking and feeling was on its way. The prerequisite for this was, of course, a healthy economy. This new furniture was primarily aimed at the young yuppie generation. For those who had both the desire and the means to invest in unique, signed furniture by famous designers. So Jonas Bohlin's concrete chair and rusty cupboard, Slottsbacken, came to be sold at Bukowski's auction house for fantastic amounts only a decade later.

The good economy and the newly awakened interest in the idea of design also meant that established furniture designers could continue to work in a more liberated way with high-class products. Few flats were built during this epoch, but rather more offices, for the new media people who were taking possession of the world at an increasing speed. The furniture was brought from Lindau & Lindekrantz/Lammhults, Börge Lindau/Blå Station (both producers of functional furniture for public places), Sandin & Bülow/Materia, Åke Axelsson who bought his own factory to manufacture his chairs, Björn Hultén, Ulla Christiansson, Thomas Sandell, Love Arbén amongst others. Many furnished complete office environments and, above all, restaurants, which led to the ordinary consumer being made aware of the quality in so-called off-furniture. Demand grew.

John Kandell experienced a new heyday when he designed furniture for Källemo, whose design-interested owner Sven Lundh also engaged young talents like Jonas Bohlin and Mats Theselius. Like Jonas Bohlin, Mats Theselius first became celebrated for a speculative armchair, made of woven birch-bark on a framework of shining aluminium. A cult chair.

A large number of female furniture designers, more interested than men in the needs of the home, made their appearance for the first time. Kerstin Olby of Olby Design, and Beban Nord and Ann Morsing of Box Design, combined Swedish tradition with modern functional form in their pale glazed furniture, sometimes in combination with limestone from Öland. Karin Tyrefors, Marie Norell, Gunilla Norin and Gunilla Allard produced personal and very serviceable furniture. The former interior design journalist, Anika Reuterswärd, managed to modernise Swedish furniture classics for Fogia, in a way that appealed to many.

Galleries and magazines inspire

More and more designers now choose to work for their own companies, so that they can take commissions from different customers. Furniture galleries were opened and exhibitions held. The magazines write diligently about both designers and furnishing in general, which quickly leads to interior design becoming an interest for the average man. "Everyone" wants to live in a split-level apartment with a loft, New York-style. One learns to mix new and old, an interest in antiques spreads from the traditional wealthy, older connoisseur to ordinary young people. It fits the newly rich crowd like a glove.

Interest in furniture and styles increases, one wants to learn more. New interior design magazines grow up like mushrooms, and home exhibitions attract multitudes. The first large home exhibition, Bo 85, with furnished conceptual houses and flats in apartment blocks, is held in Upplands Väsby in 1985. Svensk Form (Swedish Design) distinguishes itself with a post-modern flat furnished with columns, unexpected details and new spatial concepts. But there is also a well-planned ecological house, designed by White architects, exhibited here.

Even IKEA latches onto the 1980s design trend, instituting design grants, hiring more qualified designers and supplying their furniture with designer names. Also a way of shaking off the everlasting complaints about plagiarism. Svensk Form's design awards are instituted in 1984. A number of objects from different areas of use were chosen by a jury on the initiative of graphic designer HC

Above: Even old painting techniques became of interest and were used in new, post-modern ways. This marbled blue, formerly grey, TV stands like a work of art in the bookshelf.

Left: Svensk Form showed a controversial flat furnished in post-modern spirit at the Home Exhibition in 1985. Amongst other things there were pillars, marbled in Egyptian fashion, wall areas of linoleum and a dark cassette ceiling.

Below: The Englishman Tom Dixon experimented with bouancy in his S-chair made of cane and latex bands on a steel framework. This one is made for Cappellini.

Right: At the beginning of the decade, those who could afford it invested in loft living in high-tech buildings or large open-plan houses. Jan Svefors, from Magasin för Svenska Hem, lived during the 1980s in this glass-walled house with a view over Lake Vättern. The glass walls give it the feel of an exhibition hall. The view during the day is dazzling.

Above: The living room is airy and white, with a large, soft carpet and many revolving and foldable armchairs, Media, designed by Jan Dranger. Small, light tables and the many plants contribute to a summery feeling.

Left: On the other side of the stairs which lead down to the entrance hall is the dining area with its elegant, black furniture: Frame chairs and table, designed by Björn Alge. The colour scheme is black-white-grey, with red slats on the chairs like exclamation marks.

Ericson and Svensk Form. The coveted label, Utmärkt Svensk Form (Excellent Swedish Design), has been hung annually on 70–80 representative products, from furniture and home utensils to trucks and graphic design.

Unique craftsmanship also undergoes a renaissance. The glass artists Ulrica Hydman-Vallien, Bertil Vallien, Gunnel Sahlin, Anne Nilsson, Ann Wåhlström and others from KostaBoda and Orrefors again make Swedish glass world famous. Signe Persson-Melin and Karin Björquist provide us with unforgettable pottery. The Ergonomi-design Group (Ergonomic Design) makes Sweden a leader in the field of well thought-out everyday design for the functionally disabled.

Influences come from foreign furniture shows, particularly Milan. The Frenchman Philippe Starck's softly pointed forms both amused and disturbed, amongst these the three-legged chairs for the Elysée Palace and Café Costes. We are probably best acquainted with his other three-legged creation – the lemon squeezer on high spider's legs. The Italians Vico Magistretti, with his "horse blanket", Alessandro Mendini, Gaetano Pesce and others made soft sofas and chairs for different companies. The Englishman Jasper Morrison's pure, Nordic furniture, made for Vitra and Cappellini, was the most suitable for our own market. He too became famous because of a chair – the furniture designer's admission test? – the Thinking Man's Chair, in 1987, an armchair with an elegantly sloping frame of iron tubing, and a seat and back of metal lacing.

Renovation was more typical of the 1980s than new construction, at any rate at the end of the decade, when interest rates shot up, the stock market slumped and many people's finances collapsed like a house of cards. It was a decade that started with giddy consumption and ended in a hangover. Compact living became the height of fashion – and maybe a necessary evil. People lived confined and small-scale, with the necessary appendages of urban, mobile life. At this same time large public projects were completed, but their over-decorated, Post-modern glass and pastel-coloured marble facades already began to seem outdated.

"My Home is My Hotel"

When Sven Lundh began life on his own, he decided to live as if at a hotel. No unnecessary belongings, no wardrobes for "storing" things, no cooking.

He found the house, both as intellectual stimulation and undemanding way of living, in the architect John Kandell's 6,5 x 6,5 metres cubic building, which Kandell had already designed in the 1950s for himself and his wife Ulla.

"It finally got built now, in 1997," relates Sven Lundh, "but John and I have had thorough discussions about it since 1990. Since I have had a long-term co-operation with him and produced so much of his furniture, I see this small blue and white storehouse as a homage to John Kandell. It is mostly furnished with his 1980s furniture."

The white cube with its ultramarine lower half and tarred-felt roof is situated right behind Sven Lundh's office and exhibition hall for Källemo Möbler in Värnamo. As if someone had just put it down temporarily on the lawn between the tall birch trees.

The house is closed from view but yet amiably open. Five doors lead out from the only room of the lower floor. Outside the kitchen door is a patio with chairs and a small table, shaded and protected from rain by a steeply sloping roof. The upper floor has low windows, lurking high up just under the black-tarred eaves. There are no drainpipes but instead two rectangular copper chutes that stick out far beyond the sides of the house, with water barrels below.

The bottom storey has a heated clinker floor, whilst on the upper storey the floor is made of pine planks, treated with soap and wax. A galvanised spiral staircase leads up to the bedroom, workroom and the generous bathroom. All the walls of the house have white glazed panelling, which in direct sunlight assumes an almost pale pink hue. The house itself is built of concrete blocks, made in a special size to harmonise with the building's own proportions.

Left: The room on the bottom storey is built on verticals, with five tall French windows and five Pilaster shelves on the walls. The room has panelled walls and a heated clinker floor. The Pilaster shelf and the red chair, Fax, are designed by John Kandell.

Above, left: On the upper storey Sven Lundh has furnished his study and work room with both newer and older furniture designed by Bruno Mathsson, also an earlier collaborator. The white lamp Is by the Dane, Hans Wegner.

Above, right: A galvanised spiral staircase leads up to the second floor.

Previous spread: The cubic house with the ultramarine lower part looks like a small work of art amongst the birches at Värnamo. The ridge and eaves of the roof are covered with tarred roofing-felt, and rectangular drainpipes stick straight out.

The bottom storey is linked together and separated at the same time by a monumental, brick open fireplace in the middle of the house. It faces the suite comprising John Kandell's furniture and a leather sofa by Erik Karlström. Sven has placed the John Kandell table, Solitär, in the other corner, where it serves both as working table and dining table, if there is company. The kitchen is in the opposite corner – small and functional, like a hotel kitchenette with a chair and a round table for morning coffee placed at the back of the open fireplace. In the "tramp's corner".

Living like this has its advantages, according to Sven Lundh. He is still fully active – although a pensioner – with his huge on-going project, the art museum Vandalorum, in the middle of the forests of Småland, as well as his own furniture company Källemo, where his son Erik has officially been boss for some years. He takes most of

Above: Sven Lundh has a long table for work, or meals, opposite the kitchen. The table, like the other furniture in the picture, is designed by John Kandell, the Nestor, in the mid- and late 1980s. The narrow mahogany cupboard, Solitär, was already in production in the 1950s.

Right: The single room on the bottom floor is divided by a monumental open fireplace, around which the different parts of the room are grouped: sitting area to the right with chairs, table and stool by John Kandell and a sofa by Erik Karlström. There is a galvanised spiral staircase in the corner and to the left, behind the fireplace, a glimpse of the kitchen area.

his meals at Källemo, where he also watches TV and stores the books and the art he has banished from the house. When his own dream of being an artist evaporated, he took to collecting art and has accumulated a great deal through the years.

His artistic eye and intellectual attitude to objects has, instead, made him a unique furniture producer. It was Sven who discovered Jonas Bohlin, for example, and his Concrete chair at the Konstfack student exhibition in 1981.

"It gave me a real kick, because this wasn't a piece of furniture. It was an idea. It had all the qualities that consumer testing cannot cope with," says Sven Lundh with gentle sarcasm. "With due respect to consumer testing, but today all furniture is presumed to have a decent basic quality, so now it's time to affirm the quality that resides in the eye and the feelings of the viewer."

Sven Lundh is himself really delighted in Mats Theselius's latest armchair, El Rey, made of brass and embossed crocodile leather.

"It is so enticingly equivocal. A delicacy, in the form of an outrageously expensive luxury chair, a hundred percent kitsch!"

The chair has sold unexpectedly well, to the surprise of the company. Otherwise it is Pilaster, the tall, narrow bookshelf, that supports the Källemo company. They have sold 30,000 copies since John Kandell designed it in 1989.

The Design Journalist's Kitchen

Jill Dufwa has worked for the magazine Femina for several decades. It is impossible to guess how many articles about interior design she has written in that time. But you could count them, because all the issues of the magazine are up in her attic, properly bound. You just have to sit down, browse through and count them. Femina with its interior decorators, Anika Reuterswärd and Jill Dufwa, virtually "invented" modern interior design journalism in Sweden, building on simple functional and aesthetic solutions that became known as the Femina style. Unforgettable articles began to appear at the end of the 1960s and beginning of the 1970s, about renovating the kitchen, planning for children, furnishing the living room and combining furniture and objects in an aesthetic way. Femina also took part in home exhibitions.

As can be expected, Jill Dufwa herself lives amongst her favourite objects. Chairs, tables and sofas by our most famous designers, stylistically pure curtain and Venetian blind arrangements, or no curtains at all, and with the odd colour accent.

The family moved into a square Functionalist building in Bromma in 1984. The previous owner had already done large scale renovating. Amongst other things, the kitchen, scullery and maid's room had been knocked into one large, airy kitchen with room for a lot of cupboards and working surfaces. Three supporting pillars were left in the middle of the room as a personal and "youthful" accent. A new, plastic floor, from Forshaga, with discreet grey patterns and self-adhesive tiles was laid. The walls and cupboard

Left: The wall next to the dining area was covered with mirrors "so that we could get in a view of the lake"! It also makes an exciting eye-catcher with its beautiful glass objects on glass shelves. The elegant, foldable wire sofa is designed by Antti Nurmesniemi, the chairs by Niels Jörgen Haugesen and the table by Lindau & Lindekrantz for Lammhults.

Above: A large part of the short wall of the living room is taken up by Titti Fabiani's book-shelf, with square-framed, mesh-patterned glass.

Previous spread: The spacious kitchen was once kitchen, scullery and maid's room. Three supporting pillars were left. The 35-year-old cupboards were painted light grey and the wall cupboards white, while the floor was laid with patterned plastic tiles from Forshaga.

doors, from the floor up to 90 cm, were painted in light grey while everything else was white. The idea was to join the kitchen's different parts with a grey "band", whilst the white above would give a feeling of space and reflected light. The laminated working surfaces were replaced by long work boards and splash-guards of white/grey Cararra marble – a common feature in old Bromma houses.

When the family moved in during the 1980s, the floor of the living room was covered by a thick, white carpet. The long sectional

sofa, placed on the short side of the living room, was covered with the cotton fabric Jamaica, designed by Birgitta Hahn for the 10-Group. The sofa was later replaced, while the white armchairs are still there, as are the Aalto chairs with their plaited seats.

The living room and the original dining room are now one, with an open fireplace where the previous dividing-wall stood. Large windows facing in three directions let in a generous amount of light, as does the French window which opens onto a spacious terrace. A glass wall in the dining room area has been screened off by a width of starched, white cloth, which hangs from a railing on the ceiling. This gives a restful background and beautiful light. The rest of the wall is taken up by Titti Fabiani's white bookshelf with cubic compartments behind glass doors. Here books can be kept free of dust.

In contrast to most people who have "furnished once and for all", it is part of Jill Dufwa's work to change, keep up with the times, and test new ideas. Naturally this has left an impression in her own home, which changes character and becomes something of a mirror for the contemporary design debate. Occasionally it looks like a real building site, since the best studio for photographing interiors is a real home with natural light from windows facing in different directions.

"It's lucky that I have an understanding husband," says Jill Dufwa.

Right: Jill Dufwa furnished the living room of the family home in the 1980s with a mixture of extant and new. A classic Aalto-chair with plaited seat, white 1930s armchairs and a Jörgensensofa, covered with Birgitta Hahn's fabric Jamaica. The white carpet was here when the family bought the house, but has since been replaced by a sanded and oiled parquet floor.

1990–2000

Ecology, minimalism and commercial culture

The last decade of the second millennium will go down in history as the one in which it was discovered that the earth's resources were not unlimited. It was no longer possible to squeeze out the oils and minerals from the earth for immediate consumption without thought of re-growth.

We have learnt a lot, but much remains to be learnt and, above all, remedied. Politicians talk about ecology and environmental considerations, but juggernaut lorries still continue to criss-cross continents to achieve the cheapest way of assembling two components, to deliver convenience food or package biscuits – everything to earn a short-term profit. Nevertheless there are now laws against dangerous emissions and harmful substances, and to ensure that furniture and apparatuses must be deconstructed and re-used, and that one must build with "healthy" materials, and so on.

This has given designers a new perspective, and environmental arguments now carry weight, to some extent. Designer Jonas Torstensson has taken this furthest, working only with recycling – the re-use of glass, paper, tin, TV parts. In return we get drinking glasses, jugs and plates, magazine racks of cardboard, metal candlesticks and more.

Recycling cloth, old jeans, military blankets and so on, to be reincarnated as knitting thread, carpets and fabrics is not new. Rag rugs and patchwork are part of the old, agricultural Sweden where nothing was allowed to go to waste. Nowadays plastic is also ground up – packaging, PET bottles, nappy packets and advertising brochures are resurrected as shelves, stools and other useful things.

At the end of the 20th century, the computer, the Internet and the new way of communicating and living – via the screen and the mobile phone – have been the most revolutionary factors. The

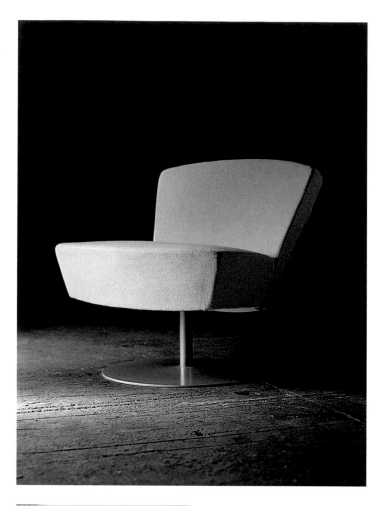

computer gives us completely new possibilities of designing, drawing buildings and quickly reaching the whole world. A world which has become the playground of young designers and media people. "The black-garbed people round Stureplan" can just as well be found on Manhattan, in San Francisco or Docklands in London. Everything reaches everybody simultaneously.

Design is simple. Super-simple

Interest in form is just as strong in the 1990s as it was in the 1920–1930s and 1950s. Buildings are built in a kind of neo-Functionalist spirit – decried by some: "copies of old Functionalism", praised by others who see a successful combination of clean surfaces, modern furnishing, light and air in the form of large balconies and floor-to-ceiling windows. They are mostly self-owned flats that are expensive, especially in attractive areas.

Certainly they are good buildings. They have large kitchens, adequate storage, good bathrooms and open-plan solutions. They are apartments that allow exciting furnishing and the flow of light from room to room. The latter in line with architect Ola Nylander's report *Bostaden som arkitektur (The Home as Architecture)* from 1998, that analyses the boundless, but important, aesthetic of the interplay of light, space and axiality in an apartment. This is far from the 1940s with its small rooms with doors that enclosed them from the tiny hall.

Since today's family no longer consists of father, mother and two children but has differing combinations and needs, there is a

Above: Claesson/Koivisto/Rune showed this simple, austere armchair, Tinto Center, at the furniture exhibition at the beginning of 2000. Made of cold-pressed foam, it is typical of the spirit of the age. Manufactured by Offect.

Left: Interest in both plastic and the 1950s is back at the end of the 20th century. Marc Newson's yellow plastic chair, Bucky, is related to the 1950s bat-chair, originally of anonymous Brazilian design in the 1930s, later manufactured by Knoll.

Right: Gunilla Allard's co-operation with Lammhults has resulted in one brilliant piece of furniture after the other. Here, the wheeled table, Chicago, with shelves of glass, laminate and leather, and the "semi-cylinder" upholstered sofa of the same name.

demand for alternative flats: large-small, open-closed, flexible walls, combined kitchen-living room, sleeping alcoves, lofts, glass-enclosed areas. It has once again become fun to be an architect, after the stagnation in building at the end of the 1980s. Lack of housing has forced the creation of new housing areas, particularly on disused industrial land. But there is also a great deal of renovation – with whitewash paints and sound materials, linseed oil, tempera, newly-made windows with thin bars, open fireplaces etc. Specialist shops such as Byggnadsvård in Gysinge and Kulturhantverkarna have never had so many buyers of paint and old housing features as now. Amongst those who have formed much of our new housing we find architects Kjell Forshed, Gert Wingårdh, Johan Nyrén, Thomas Sandell and Love Arbén. In the spirit of this design-conscious age, one is trying to reinstate the total view of housing, both indoors and outdoors, that was so self evident for the 1930s Functionalists, but which contemporary administration, building policies and lack of trust have sabotaged. A flagrant example is the Modern Museum in Stockholm by Rafael Moneo, the Spaniard, about which even the most insignificant local politician had an opinion and which ended up as neither one thing nor the other.

0-design or baroque – which will rule?

Even designers cross boundaries. It is not individual objects that are important but rather a whole "design concept". There are new dimensions of both humanism and intellectualism in the design. But mostly it is minimalism that dominates at the end of the 1990s and the start of 2000. Soon style can not be simplified further without self-imploding and resulting in a kind of o-design. Mies van der Rohe's expression Less is More has become Less is Bore or Nothing is All, depending on how you see it. Carl-Gustaf Petersén, head of Bukowskis, the auction company, writing in Elle magazine about this cold intellectual trend, adds: "If minimalism continues we will get a super-minimalism that will drive even Calvinists to tremble with longing for a floral armchair in front of the open fireplace!"

At the same time this decade of design has, of course, produced an abundance of excellent form. A glass designer like the purist Ingegerd Råman has at last received full recognition. Her milli-metre-conceived glass is found in both the Swedish Embassy and ordinary homes. Carina Seth-Andersson has also achieved international fame with her rectangular bowls and dishes of clear glass. Ceramist Kennet Williamsson makes subtle, fragile plates and bowls,

Above: Simple shapes and bright colours dominate end-of-the-century furnishing. This flat was exhibited at H99 in Helsingborg, with a white sofa by Helene Tiedemann and a red carpet by Pia Wallén.

Left: Not much happens in fabric printing; there is a preference for working with textures. Bigitta Hahn's Stockholm's fabrics are an exception, here with the pattern, Sergels torg.

Below: Kersti Sandin and Lars Bülow, with their company Materia, have full control over all stages of production. In-house designs, factory, advertising and sales guarantee quality. This sofa, Arketyp, received Svensk Form's design award in 1993.

Above: The productive trio Mårten Claesson/Eero Koivisto/Ola Rune produces a torrent of furniture and fittings. They designed a series of solid-upholstered furniture on metal frames for Scandiform. This armchair, Dropp, is one of them.

Left: Craftsmanship regains respect, and many designers look for new solutions based on classical ideals. One of them is ceramist Ingela Karlsson, who deftly creates new designs with influences from Baroque and 18th century.

Below, left: One of the latest creations that Mats Theselius makes for Källemo is the armchair, El Rey. "A real delicacy, with its combination of kitsch and expense," says Sven Lundh, Källemo's owner. It has immediately achieved cult status and the waiting list is long.

Signe Persson-Melin and Ingela Karlsson experiment with ceramics on the cusp between functional and baroque. Pia Törnell works in a stylistically pure and original way with china for Rörstrands. Tom Hedqvist continues to design stripes for the 10-Group and Birgitta Hahn has created eye-catching fabrics with Stockholm motifs. Maria Åström and Anna Sörensson are among our best pattern designers while Gunilla Lagerhem-Ullberg creates utilitarian and Svensk Form Design-awarded carpets for Kasthall. Pia Wallén has always been one step ahead with her felt accessories and clothes, which later have become an international trend.

On the handcraft side, however, things have stood still. Admittedly, Liljevalchs do have two inspiring and critically acclaimed handcraft exhibitions during the 1990s, but both must be seen as resulting from the efforts of a few enthusiasts. IKEA-sponsored handcraft is also exhibited in the USA, where it is a success.

No, the 1990s will probably be remembered primarily for its furniture and furnishings. Mostly thanks to the fact that Swedish style, both 18th century and Modern, suddenly became trendy abroad. IKEA's 18th century furniture opened the way in 1993, followed by the same company's PS-furniture two years later, in Milan. Stefan Ytterborn, a real entrepreneur in this field, held a series of design happenings in Kungsträdgården, Stockholm, under the name of Futurniture. Foreign magazines took the bait.

The biggest breakthrough for new Swedish design was at the furniture exhibition in Milan in 1998, where four companies – Asplund, Box, Cbi and David Design – together with the fashion company Ellegal/Illegal, Diesel Music and Sturehof's food became the hit of the year in this design-choosy city. "The third most important design event", wrote the magazines after tasting exotic crisp bread with whitefish roe and admiring blonde minimalism.

The direction that the "design concept" took during the 1990s resulted in a number of small, specialised stores, preferably with their own team of designers. The list is long, but Klara, Asplund, Designtorget, Design House Stockholm and David Design are some of the most interesting.

The work of many of the furniture designers of the 1990s breach boundaries: for themselves, for projects or for temporary production partners, from powerful IKEA to tiny Källemo. Architects Thomas Eriksson and Thomas Sandell assembled IKEA's PS-collection of young, designed furniture and utensils. Mattias Ljunggren, Björn Dahlström, Jonas Lindwall and others work in a spirit of neoclassical simplicity. Björn Dahlström's breadth even includes toys and cycles. Dan Ihreborn has become the doyen of upholstered furniture, as too, Gunilla Allard, who represents a new Functionalist style with her Le Corbusier-inspired but personally interpreted chairs, sofas and trolley-tables for Lammhults. A kind of public furniture for private use.

The leading lights of the new millennium are, however, Mårten Claesson, Eero Koivisto and Ola Rune. They made a newly conceived, experimental house which was exhibited on Sergel's Square, as early as 1994. If anyone has come to represent the minimalist idea of interior design it is this trio, who have fitted-out many trendy bars, chain stores and private apartments. The furnishing of the Swedish Ambassador's residence in Berlin is the jewel in their crown.

Above: Natural materials, exciting angles and large glass surfaces characterise new, preferably custom-designed, homes. This two-section house joined by a glass entrance won Hus & Hem magazine's house-of-the-year competition. Åsa Bronge Franzén is the architect.

Left: The furniture company Källemo is unique in its investment in unusual furniture with high artistic value. But it is rewarding in the long run to be exclusive and stubborn. Mats Theselius's armchair, Ambassad, one of a long series of similar ones, was chosen as Furniture of the Year 2000 by Sköna Hem magazine.

Above: Mattias Ljunggren made an orange-red wooden armchair, Gute. A modern version of Carl Larsson's furniture. In 2000, it was complemented with a light-blue chair and a large, square table with angled legs.

Left: Swedish glass continues to be prized the world over – maybe mostly for its austere purity. Per B Sundberg, Orrefors, is however, more ostentatious.

Right: The kitchen increasingly becomes the focal point of the home, at the same time as it is given the character of a restaurant kitchen. This is IKEA's version of an inexpensive, functional kitchen, situated in one corner of the living room.

H99 Summarises the Decade

Before the 20th century had ebbed away, Helsingborg held the last home exhibition of the millennium, H99 – a sequel to the renowned H55. Tall apartment blocks, with unmistakable reference to the 1920–30s and Functionalism, filled Helsingborg's waterfront. Smaller, inventive houses, built by different companies and architects, were placed further out on the pier. IKEA also exhibited an inexpensive block of flats, available for purchase through them.

A lot of positive, but also critical, things could be said about this exhibition, but the politics behind it were pungently summarised by consumer journalist Charlotte Reimersson on TV: "The flats that the building constructors present as "customer-orientated" are outrageously expensive and badly planned luxury apartments without functioning kitchens, but with room for 100 cocktail guests! And the ones that are called "efficient flats" are similarly impossible 20 square metre rooms."

There were of course also many beautiful and well thought-out flats with a sea view, some of the best designed by Danish agency Tegnestuen Vandkunsten.

Above: Like the bow of a tall ship and with 1930s-inspired balconies and rounded windows, a row of newly built apartment blocks stands along the quay in Helsingborg. They were finished in time for the exhibition H99 in the summer of 1999.

Left: Riksbyggen's luxury apartment features a large bathroom – larger than the kitchen – with sauna, balcony and a sea view. The bathtub is designed by Philippe Starck.

Previous spread: The luxury flat at the top of Riksbyggen's building at H99 has a sea view on three sides. The large room is 100 square metres, with surround windows and an open fireplace in the middle. The sofa, Hockney, and armchairs, Dropp, have been designed by the trio Claesson-Koivisto-Rune, the wide armchair at the far end is by Björn Dahlström and pouffes by Lena Bergström. The trolley table, Cargo, designed by Gunilla Allard, the storied table by Bruno Mathsson.

Above, left: Birgitta Ramdell's flat in the Danish-designed block of flats has an open-plan design, with a large hall between the kitchen/living room and workroom/guest room. There are large floor-to-ceiling windows everywhere. The airiness is manifest and exciting.

Above, right: A red Pilaster shelf marks the opening to the kitchen. At the far end, there is a dining table with Arne Jacobsen's chairs Sjuan, a black folding armchair from Börge Lindau/Blå Station and a graceful olive tree. A floor-to-ceiling window in the corner lets in light.

Right: Oiled oak ship's flooring with black seams makes this flat an aesthetic experience in itself. The balcony cuts into the flat and feels like a natural part of the living room. The furniture is a mixture of old and new, and features Danish leather-covered armchairs.

Ecology and luxury side by side

Architects Thomas Sandell and Anders Landström presented a developed version of their timber house Vistet, shown in Stockholm a year earlier. This small weekend cottage of 27 square metres + a 13 square metre loft is built of horizontal timbers and without insulation. It is painted with pearl-grey calcimine on the outside and egg-oil tempera on the inside. The furnishing is by Norrgavel. Vistet is infused with ecological thinking and functional solutions.

The opposite could be seen in the luxury apartment, with the whole of the Sound at its feet, and balconies in three different directions. 180 square metres distributed through four rooms, a mini-kitchen and a colossal bath-sauna department. The living room alone was 100 square metres in this apartment, planned for a childless professional couple. The building contractor was Riksbyggen, and Tangram the architect.

Birgitta Ramdell, responsible for planning the exhibition area, lived in an attractive and realistic flat. This HSB flat, designed by Tegnestuen Vandkunsten, is 90 square metres, with three rooms and a large balcony. The kitchen is integrated with the living room, and the open hall can be used as a library. Large windows let in a great deal of light and even afford a view of the sea, despite the flat's location in the rear of the building.

Left: Looking out from the compact kitchen corner of the timber house Vistet, towards the main room which has a dining area in one corner and a sitting and reading area in the other.

Above: The timber walls are massive enough to insulate the house. The tall soapstone stove provides more than sufficient heat, also for the sleeping-loft. Norrgavel have done the furnishing.

Above: This small timbered house, Vistet, contains everything two people need in a weekend cottage. It is cubic in shape, 5,5 x 5,5 x 5,5 metres, including a loft. The materials are old, reliable eight inch timber, top-to-tail and without insulation. Grass on the roof.

Right: The loft takes up half the area one storey up. There is a 120 cm bed on one side and a narrower one on the other side. The walls and grey floor are painted with pleasantly smelling linseed oil paints.

Environmentally Approved Living

The demand for ecological thinking and a healthy, non-toxic environment increased during the 1990s. Justifiably so, since mass-produced products bring with them unknown conservation methods, metal components, consistency additives and so on which unquestionably affect people.

Much has been done during the last decade of the 20th century to minimise emissions. Ideas about recycling and re-use are built into the product from the beginning.

Furniture designer Nirvan Richter and his company Norrgavel have taken it upon themselves to manufacture furniture and accessories, from an environmentally aware starting point. His furniture was, at the turn of the millennium, one of the few Swedish products to be given the environmental label, Svanen.

"We only use natural materials and work with Swedish wood," he relates. "Pine, birch, alder, oak, beech, and cherry."

He would rather let furniture, walls or textiles remain untreated or use less durable, but environment-friendly, paints and treatments, selling the beauty of wear and tear as an ecological argument. Ovolin's egg-oil tempera, for example, dries slowly and is sensitive until it has "settled" properly, but then produces a rock-hard surface. The paints contain no toxic solvents or preservatives. However, they must be treated as perishables owing to their organic constituents. The unified colour ranges are mild and robust at the same time. One seems to discern the colour ideas of the anthroposophists. All the textiles and coverings are in linen of different thickness. Milis Ivarsson is Norrgavel's colour consultant.

Nirvan Richter is not interested in furniture as individual products. It is a wholeness, a kind of spiritual living that interests him. He has created, with architect Kjell Forshed, two show-flats where both their ideas can be summarised in the philosopher Wittgenstein's thesis: Beauty is immeasurable and personal. It is purely a question of the relation between the viewer and the object. Beauty can never be described in words, it must be experienced, and

the experience of beauty presents itself only when all the parts fit together, forming a unity.

Through the years, Nirvan Richter's interiors at different home exhibitions have attracted great interest. One of the first was at Karlskrona, where the shipyard island of Stumholmen was built with flats and where Norrgavel's furniture filled one beautiful flat. The next project, a house designed by Christer Blomqvist for Nimab at the home exhibition at Staffanstorp in 1997, was given a mixture of furniture of his own design and older classics, to give the exhibition house the feeling of being lived in. The result was an airy and harmonious house.

Nirvan Richter has developed this lived-in feeling even further in the two exhibition flats in Kjell Forshed's house on Nybodahöjden in Stockholm in 1999. The co-operation between Kjell Forshed, Nirvan Richter, Milis Ivarsson and construction company JM began at a very early stage. All the walls were given robust colours. The floor in the kitchen and dining room in one of the flats was laid with split, recycled bricks. The other floor was treated with soap. Furniture, fabrics and objects finally drew together the rooms into a kind of living-caves, where the mysterious and the spiritual were palpable. It is here that you can best experience Wittgenstein's words about beauty as a result of wholeness.

Left: The large exhibition apartment, like a penthouse with balconies on two sides, has been furnished by Nirvan Richter with furniture of his own design, and has robust colours. The floor is on two levels, with a double door out to the large terrace. Walls are painted with egg-oil tempera in a warm umber-green colour. The dining room in one half and a generous sitting area in the other.

Right: The bedroom is made for deep, relaxed sleep. Curtains, bedding and the pine panelling all have the same deep blue. All the textiles are of linen – a pleasant material for the body. The pine planks on the floor have a grey glaze.

Previous spread: Dark green-brown walls and similar drapes of rough linen also feature in the living room of the other exhibition flat in Nyboda. Notice the doorway right up to the ceiling. Nirvan Richter's sofa and easy chair are covered with elk leather in differing pale hues. The oval book table can be extended with the help of the extra shelf underneath.

The Terraced House
on the Roof

Glass artist Lena Bergström is characteristed by her speed, creativity
and rationalism, something which is reflected in the home she and
her partner Olle Johansson share, high up in an apartment block on
Karlavägen in Stockholm. The building was built by architect Kjell
Ödeen in 1959 and is surprising for its exceptionally well thought-
out features. And planning. Lena's and Olle's flat, with an entrance
from a patio-like passage, is like a terraced house up on the roof
itself. You enter via the upper storey which has a hall, kitchen and
dining area, and a 12 square metre terrace facing south.

The rest of the flat is one floor down. The staircase opens into a
large living room angled towards a working area, created by remov-
ing a partition wall. On the other side of the hall are a bedroom and
yet another workroom – the room where Lena makes her sketches.

Beauty has a very central role in everything that Lena Bergström
makes. Despite being qualified as a textile artist she has come to
work mostly with glass. Glass is quicker. You can catch the beauty
of light in it. That is why she works preferably with clear glass, with
its high demands on purity and accuracy, but which also lends itself
to breath-taking aesthetic experiences. She works for Orrefors, in
co-operation with their skilful glassblowers. Lena's glass has won
prize after prize throughout the world.

She regularly operates in the textile business, most recently for
the company Designer's Eye – with a programme of felt textiles –
and Åke Axelsson, with whom she has created the furniture range,
Spring. Åke designs the furniture and Lena the quilted felt upholstery.

There are several of her felt seat cushions for Designer's Eye in
the living room of the flat and also a tufted carpet, which she has
made for Kasthall. The armchairs are from IKEA, one covered with

Left: The dining room, reached directly from the hall, looks like a clinical clean, white cube. Light streams in through the curtainless 1950s window. Notice the elegant handles. A cord carpet from Woodnotes partly covers the grey linoleum floor. Jacobsen's chairs, 7:an, stand around a dining table covered with white oilcloth.

Above: Outside the dining area is the large south-facing terrace. Comfortable chairs, a little the worse for wear, are placed among the plants that remind Lena of their uses, of other countries or serve as inspiration.

Previous spread: The large open living room, one floor down, is happily liberated from knick-knacks. The colour scheme is white, grey, black with a little red. Lena has designed the sitting cushions and the carpet. The IKEA armchairs are re-covered with white and black felt respectively, and chairs from Vitra, designed by Charles Eames in the 1940s. The table is Finnish.

white felt, the other with black. Charles Eames has designed the black chairs, next to the open fireplace, in the 1940s. They are now manufactured by Vitra.

The whole apartment is painted white – Stockholm's white on the walls – grey and black, with the occasional splash of red. Rational aesthetics come into play here. Instead of lots of different cupboards and shelves, as there so easily are in homes, everything is loosely stuffed into white wall-cupboards from Marbodal, a decimetre up from the floor. The kitchen also has similar cupboards. This makes for uniformity and easy cleaning.

You can see the austere aesthetic dining area as soon as you enter the flat. It features a grey floor with a cord carpet from Woodnotes,

a long table covered by a shiny, white oilcloth, Arne Jacobsen's veneer chairs 7:an and curtainless 1950s window with Lena's clear glass vases on the sill.

On the other side of the work surface of black slate is the kitchen. The cupboards are white here, too, and all the objects carefully chosen to fit into the black and white colour scheme.

Colours break through only on the terrace, but in a restrained range of different greens.

"I want to get all the different 'me's' in the balcony plants," Lena explains. "Here is grass – fantastic, varied grass– in different pots. And here is useful wheat, and here is linen, which is one of my work materials. France, which I love, is here in the form of lavender, and Japan, in the form of Japanese lanterns which have beautiful orange-red flower balls until autumn."

The balcony is a real breathing space in the middle of the city, above the traffic noise, with rooftops and the sky as neighbours. This is where they have dinner, rest, sunbathe and talk. Lena thinks through all her ideas here before she goes down to the workroom to put them on paper. All the finished objects stand in a row in this room, as inspiration and as proof of her diligence. Always in transition.

Above: The same whiteness prevails in the workroom as in the other rooms. Marbodal cupboards hang on the wall, with white PS-shelves from IKEA above. A good place for Lena Bergström's own, elegant glass.

Right: The whole kitchen is white and black, even Lena Bergström's own tall vases, decoratively placed in the window. Cupboards are from Marbodal.

Converted
1940s Three-room Flat

In 1942, a block of flats was built in Östermalm, Stockholm, according to strictly rational principals. The 77 square metre three-room flat had a narrow kitchen, streamlined for one person. Every room had its own door. Corridors and double doors screened off the kitchen and bedroom from the reception area – the large, 24 square metre best room with a balcony and open fireplace. There was a "best part" and a "living part".

When Andreas Hellström and Malin Nevander bought the flat they contacted newly qualified architects Bolle Tham and Martin Videgård Hansson. Their first requirement was to let in more light, to give the flat a more airy feel. Their second requirement: a kitchen with room to socialise. Away with all the doors and passages, and the division between public and private.

Bolle Tham and Martin Videgård Hansson made a reshuffle to give the static flat a completely new dynamic. They "cut out" the eating area next to the window of the narrow kitchen, and erected a wall of laminated blasted glass beside the working surface. This created a small new room, simultaneously allowing light to pass through into the kitchen. Today this room is a workroom, soon to be transformed into a nursery. The wall between kitchen and the adjacent bedroom was removed, to make room for their dream kitchen, with generous space for both food preparation and eating. The doors and corners of the hall were also removed, so that guests now enter directly from the hall.

The idea of large open surfaces is a new way of seeing the kitchen, completely different to 1940s thinking. Today the kitchen has status. It is here that the cook demonstrates his art, here food is prepared together and friends socialise, just like at a restaurant. It is an international trend.

The other part of the reshuffle concerned the bathroom and toilet. Dividing walls were removed here also, and the bathtub was

Left: Looking from the bedroom through the clothes closet and bathroom towards the living room. The old wardrobes have been left intact.

Above: The exclusive bathtub, elevated and sunk into a surface of black slate with room for a hand basin. A washing machine is integrated in the front corner. The rest is white tiling and oiled parquet.

Previous spread: Here we see the kitchen and dining area opening into the new room, created by cutting off the dining area of the old, narrow kitchen. Everything is painted white, the parquet floors are oiled and the working surfaces are of black slate. Open shelving replaces wall cupboards.

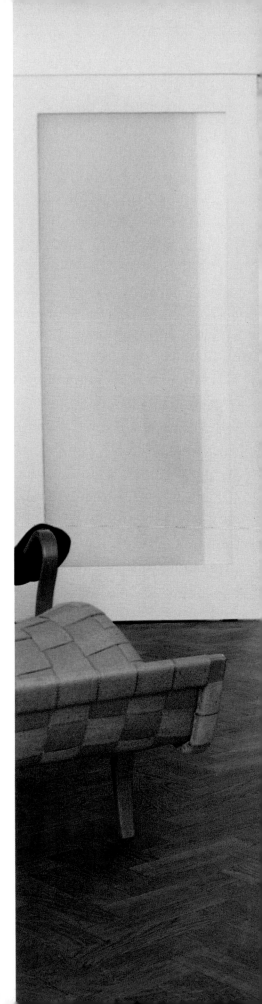

put on a plinth to raise it to the height of the hand basin. As in the kitchen, black slate is used for the surfaces, into which the bathtub and washbasin have been sunk. This gives an unusual, rather exclusive impression. The bathroom has been integrated with the living room in an almost Roman way, allowing for communication between the rooms. Two blasted glass sliding doors divide the bathroom from the living room and can be pushed aside, allowing you to lie in the bathtub and watch the blaze in the open fireplace!

Rethinking the way of living in an old flat is interesting, according to Bolle and Martin. The old solutions were seldom motivated by pleasure but were, rather, weighted by concerns for status or pure function. But the functional does not need to be lost if you open spaces, let the light flow through and integrate functions. On the contrary. We are different people today than 60 years ago, with different demands.

Above: A vertical slatted curtain hangs in front of the balcony window.

Right: The living room, not yet completely furnished, opens towards the bathroom, bedroom and hall. Two blasted glass sliding doors can be opened to provide unexpected light and space. On the right, the bathtub can be seen, one step up.

Travelling Light into the 21st Century

Has the home any further role to play? This is a question one can ask when comparing the heavy, overloaded castles for the Family with a capital and eternal F of the turn of the previous century with today's small, austere survival dens. For they are hardly more than this, these spartan one and two room flats, that can be closed up at any time when their owner goes out into the world – for a month, or a year.

Single households are on the increase; in large cities they are already in a majority. Young people put off having families. Work and travel are more important, so one cannot be tied down by possessions.

Photographer Patrik Engquist is one such travelling minimalist. He is stationed – as it is called these days – in Stockholm but has the world as his work place.

He owns a small one room flat high up in the famous communal house that Alva Myrdal initiated in her time and which was completed according to Sven Markelius's plans in 1935. It is only 27 square metres, but a window, with a long balcony, lets in light and space to make the flat seem much bigger. If it should get too crowded anyway, Patrik Engquist has both a spacious studio and a summer house in the archipelago.

Sven Markelius's spirit is "implicit" in the flat. His urban thinking led him to do away with both kitchen and food preparation. Meals were brought up in a dumb-waiter, for which this building was renowned, directly from the communal restaurant. The home was primarily a place for the working man, woman or small family to sleep in.

Left and above: The dining corner is totally white apart from the cedar table, designed by Claesson-Koivisto-Rune, which can be extended to double length. Peter Karpf has designed the white moulded chairs. Flooring is the original cement terrazzo, previously covered with linoleum. Lighting in the form of strip lights in the corner and along the ceiling.

Previous spread: From the outer door, looking straight into the small flat, which has been given an almost magic feeling of space due to the light from the large window, and the gently curved white, cupboard wall. The sofa-bed is on the left and the wall behind the TV bench has the flat's sole, striking painting by Brian Wendleman.

Design trio Mårten Claesson-Eero Koivisto-Ola Rune have helped Patrik Engquist to transform the flat into a trendy, contemporary living space for one person. The functionalist shell with its clean transitions between floor, walls and ceiling has been retained. No romantic skirting-boards or copings; everything is matter-of-fact austere.

A wall of pleasantly curved wardrobes, which also serves to obscure the staircase wall cutting into the room, is the real boost for the flat. The cupboard doors are floor-to-ceiling, fitting closely to each other, without handles. Admittedly almost impossible to open, but as Patrik Engquist says: looks count most! Painted in matt white, like the rest of the flat, the metal doors look more like wood. The original cement, somewhat speckled, terrazzo floor was revealed on removal of the 1930s linoleum. The door and small stump of wall in the minimal kitchen corner were removed, also the door to the food corner. Everything is open.

Claesson-Koivisto-Rune have designed the furniture in their unmistakable linear style. Sofa-bed in the middle of the room, an extendable dining table, TV bench with room for bed linen, kitchen and bathroom fittings. Cedar is the all-pervading material, even for the sink, hand basin in the bathroom and the tall, upright bathtub! Very beautiful, but maybe not without problems. Inspiration came from Japan where bathtubs have long been made of cedar, which is supposedly mould-resistant.

The small bathroom, with its heated clinker floor and white-tiled walls, stands like a cube in the middle of the flat. A small red window opens towards the dining area, giving a striking light outwards.

Lighting is an important feature. Here it consists of long, connected fluorescent tubes, under the ceiling, along the walls, and down to the floor in the eating corner and behind the TV bench. Brightness is controlled with a central dimmer.

Sound is important, too. A black Bang & Olufsen stands in sole majesty on the TV bench, while the wardrobe beside it contains a sound system worth a small fortune.

Above: Looking from the TV corner towards the kitchen, bathroom and eating area. the bathroom stands like a cube in the middle of the wall. Notice the doorway right up to the ceiling. A small red window glows on the wall towards the dining area which is lit by a vertical strip light.

Left: The old dumb-waiter to the communal restaurant is preserved in the corner of the kitchen. Otherwise: a stove plate and stainless steel oven. The sink, working surfaces and cupboard doors are all made of cedar.

Above: Claesson-Koivisto-Rune have specially designed the hand basin and bathtub in cedar for the small bathroom, with elegant taps. The mirror above the hand basin transforms into a red-tinted window facing out to the dining area.

Bibliography

Bergqvist, Michelsen & E:son Lindman: *Josef Frank Falsterbovillorna.* Arkitektur förlag 1998

Bergström, Birgitta & Fornander, Karin: *Från funkis till bas* (essay). 1997

Blockmakarens hus. Stockholms stadsmuseum 1996

Bodén, *Christer: Modernismens arkitektur.* Archi Libris 1997

Borelius Brodd, Anna m fl: *Thun-Olle; Olof Thunström – en folkhemmets arkitekt.* Byggförlaget 1999

Boman, Monica m fl: *Svenska möbler 1890–1990.* Signum 1991

Byggnaders särdrag. Boverket 1995

Christiansson, Carl: *Bruno Mathsson.* Raster 1993

Design för maskinen. Katalog till Museet för Industridesign, Bångbro 1999

Ferretti, Gianpaolo: *Alvar Aalto.* Cosmit Milano 1998

Fiell, Charlotte & Peter: *1000 Chairs.* Taschen 1997

Hem. Stockholms stadsmuseum 1994

Henriksson-Abelin, Kerstin: *Sätta bo.* Rabén & Sjögren 1962

Hultin, Olof m fl: *Guide till Stockholms arkitektur.* Arkitektur förlag 1998

Husmoderns bok, om kök och köksinredningar. Åhlén & Åkerlunds förlag 1927

Jor, Finn & Havran, Jiri: *Hemma hos författare, konstnärer och kompositörer i Norden.* Prisma 1999

Larsson, Lena & Svedberg, Elias: *Heminredning.* När-var-hur serien, Forum 1965

Le Corbusier (catalogue). Mjällby konstgård 1993

Lundahl, Gunilla: *John Kandell.* Raster 1993

Nathorst-Böös, Thomas: *BostadsBoken.* Hyresgästföreningen 1999

Nylander, Ola: *Bostaden som arkitektur.* Chalmers 1998

Paulsson, Gregor, Asplund, Gunnar, Gahn, Wolter, Markelius, Sven, Sundahl, Eskil & Åhrén, Uno:
    acceptera. Tiden 1931, re-printed 1980

Paulsson, Gregor: *Vackrare vardagsvara.* Svenska slöjdföreningen 1919

Rudberg, Eva: *Stockholmsutställningen.* Stockholmia förlag 1930

Rörby, Martin: *En miljon bostäder.* Arkitekturmuseets årsbok 1996

Seklets spegel. Exhibition catalogue, Stockholm as European Cultural Capital 1999

Sommar, Ingrid: *Stockholm Modern.* Wahlström & Widstrand 1998

Sparke, Penny: *Design – 1900-talets pionjärer.* Bonniers 1998

Svensk byggnadskonst under 1900-talet. Arkitekturmuseum 1993

Tambini, Michael: *1900-talets design.* Wahlström & Widstrand 1998

Thunander, Britt och Ingemar: *Svensk stilhistoria.* Bonnier fakta 1983

Tidskriften *Byggnadskultur* (various issues). Svenska föreningen för byggnadsvård

Topelius, Annsofi: *Skönhet för alla och Ellen Keys Strand.* Östergötlands museum 1982

Wagner, Otto: *Vår tids byggnadskonst.* Wien 1914 och Byggförlaget 2000

Vi husmödrar. 1956–1962

Wickman, Kerstin m fl: *100 år av designhistoria.* Svensk Form 1997

Wickman, Kerstin m fl: *Formens rörelse.* Carlssons förlag 1995

Östberg, Ragnar: *Ett hem.* Verdandis småskrifter 1913

Index

Numbers in *italics* refer to photo captions